SURVIVAL TIPS

150 WAYS TO SURVIVE EMERGENCY SITUATIONS

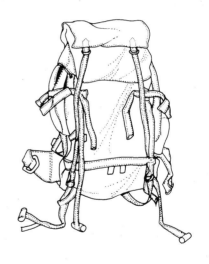

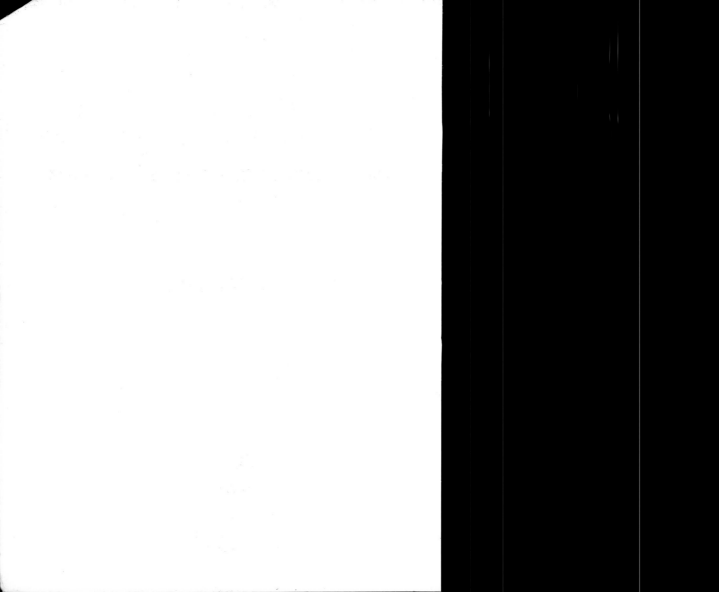

SURVIVAL TIPS

150 WAYS TO SURVIVE EMERGENCY SITUATIONS

CLIVE JOHNSON

THE LYONS PRESS

GUILFORD, CONNECTICUT
AN IMPRINT OF THE GLOBE PEQUOT PRESS

First Lyons Press edition, 2002
Copyright © 2002 by Amber Books Ltd

The Lyons Press is an imprint of The Globe Pequot Press.

Editorial and design by
Amber Books Ltd
Bradley's Close
74–77 White Lion Street
London N1 9PF

Project Editor: Chris Stone
Design: Hawes Design
All illustrations courtesy of Anne Cakebread, Patrick Mulrey, and Tony Randell

2   4   6   8   10   9   7   5   3   1

The Library of Congress Cataloging-in-Publication Data is available on file.

ISBN 1-58574-567-7

Printed in Singapore

CONTENTS

INTRODUCTION

Survival is based on simple principles, which include basic survival skills. But these skills alone will not save your life – it is your mental attitude and determination that will ultimately determine whether you live or die.

In survival situations, the will to survive is all-important. Ultimately, your mind controls your body, and when the mind gives up, the body will fail to survive. If your mental attitude is wrong, then no amount of survival knowledge or training will save you. Without doubt, the most important aids to survival are the abilities to remain calm and optimistic, and to concentrate the mind and adapt to the new situation.

In real-life survival situations, the desire to 'get out' can be so strong that it takes over all conscious thought, creating a self-defeating frame of mind. Thoughts of home and family fill the mind, driving people to a state of mental hopelessness. In normal life, we are surrounded by everything we need to live in comfort. In an emergency situation, all the trappings and comforts of modern living can be unexpectedly stripped away, forcing us to adapt (both mentally and physically) to primitive ways of staying alive.

PSYCHOLOGICAL PROBLEMS THAT WILL AFFECT YOUR CHANCES OF SURVIVAL

ANXIETY

This is a sense of impending disaster, which can be brought on in a survival environment by the difficulties of finding basic needs. Symptoms may include palpitations, stabbing pains in the chest and difficulty in breathing, sighing and over-breathing. There may also be muscle tension, pains in the back and a tendency to grasp things too tightly. Other symptoms may include dry mouth, diarrhoea, nausea, belching and difficulty in swallowing. External symptoms may include pallor, sweating and yawning.

Anxiety will reduce performance if steps are not taken to counter it. The best short-term way of coping is to try to identify the particular problems causing the anxiety. Write them down and deal with them one by one. As you deal with the problems that are making you anxious, you are likely to become more confident and less anxious.

DEPRESSION

Depression can involve a feeling of hopelessness or inability to cope, perhaps in the face of overwhelming difficulties or repeated failure. Anxiety can be linked to depression, and the symptoms in many people involve slowing down and listlessness.

Depression can be made worse by feelings of guilt or personal fault, especially where there is little reassurance to the contrary. A depressed person may feel that anyone else would have performed better in particular circumstances. This may result from over-competitive or dominating behaviour by others. A cure for this negative way of thinking is for the depressed person to think about and develop their personal gifts and to take sensible measures in dealing with weaknesses.

Depression is common and should be viewed as something that will pass away. Remember that even great men suffer from depression: Winston Churchill (Britain's Prime Minister during the Second World War) called it his 'black dog', but he did not allow it to grip him for too long. Try and view your depression dispassionately and do not let it grow roots. Let it pass away.

STRESS

It is natural to suffer stress in a survival environment, especially one that has involved any kind of accident. Stress is the body's natural way of dealing with problems that require urgent reactions – indeed, in the right circumstances, it will improve performance. If the stress factor continues for a long period, however, the body's reactions become very tiring and this actually reduces the ability of the individual to cope. Exposure to stressful situations can cause symptoms of anxiety or depression, such as palpitations, indigestion and muscular aches and pains.

The best way to deal with stress is to attempt to control it. This is difficult: you will feel a strong urge to let the body's reactions rule you and you may lose your composure. However, your ability to control it will improve with practice. When circumstances allow, make a conscious effort to calm your racing mind and to slow your physical movements (unless, of course, you are in an emergency, such as a fire, where you need to think and move very fast). Identify the problems that are stressing you, itemize them and set about dealing with them one by one.

Mood swings are often a natural part of an outdoor survival situation when people are tired or under pressure, so be cautious about making snap diagnoses and possibly alienating a member of your group. However, displays of uncharacteristic behaviour among your party members may well signal that it is time to stop and rest, giving everyone physical and mental rest and recuperation.

Remember – no matter how bad the situation is, the only things that will get you out of the predicament are your skills combined with both your physical and mental abilities.

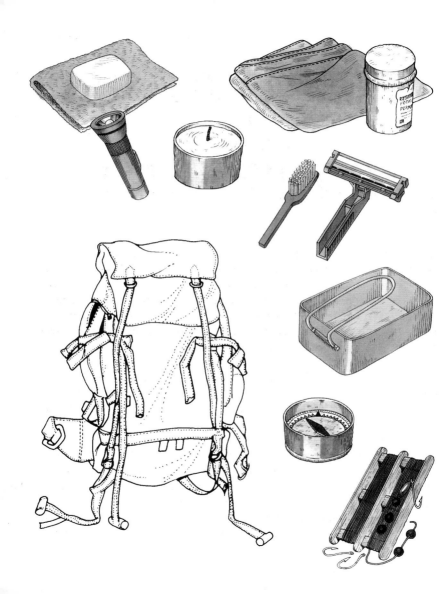

PREPARATION AND EQUIPMENT

Don't Panic! The shock of being cut off from the usual supports of civilization – from food, water, shelter, warmth and companionship – will vary according to your circumstances and training. Whatever your background or however well prepared for the situation in which you find yourself, it is vitally important to get over the initial trauma as quickly as possible. Always remember that the situation you are in is perhaps no different to those that men and women have known – and survived – for centuries, even to this day.

Remain calm; do not allow panic to cloud the mind. You may not be aware of it, but you already have the necessary qualities to survive – determination, perseverance, ingenuity and humour. All you need to do now is to mentally adapt to your new circumstances. You may not be used to having to go out and forage for food or to locate sources of water. But remember that the qualities and skills you use in finding and holding down a job, and in negotiating the best deal for yourself and your family in your daily life, are similar to those that men and women have used to find shelter, warmth and food for themselves and their families.

As you adapt and begin to take sensible precautions in a well-planned way, you will find that your mind and body will adjust as far as possible to the new environment. Your senses, somewhat dulled by urban comforts, will become sharper and your mind will focus and begin preparing a survival plan. As long as you maintain a strong will to survive, you will overcome setbacks and begin to master your environment.

1. EMPOWER THE MIND

Finding yourself in unfamiliar surroundings with none of the comforts of normal life and with the ever-present threat of death can produce high levels of personal stress. Special services personnel use a form of self-hypnosis to help them perform a kind of internal 'battleproofing'. The technique involves breathing-based meditation and self-suggestion that allows the heartbeat to slow down as well as the blood pressure to drop. This effectively reduces the symptoms of anxiety, which in turn leads the mind to feel more balanced and restored.

The soldier can imagine himself coping with those situations he fears. The human mind is remarkable in that it cannot tell the difference between events that are vividly imagined and those that are actually experienced. Thus a soldier who is, say, particularly afraid of artillery fire can, to a large degree, 'inoculate' himself against what is known as Combat Stress reaction. Anyone can use the same technique to overcome anxiety and the stress of finding yourself on the edge of survival.

Try to keep your mind active all the time by thinking of things you wish to do in the future. Develop mental projects for yourself – for example, write a novel in your head, dreaming up a new chapter each day, or plan a business idea.

To be a survivor, the following personal qualities give you an advantage:

● The ability to concentrate the mind and improvise.
● To adapt to the situation while remaining calm.
● To remain optimistic, while at the same time preparing for the worst.

● Being able to understand, then deal with and overcome your own fears and worries.

2. WHAT TO DO FIRST

You are cold, wet, hungry and may be injured; there may also be injured people and dead bodies around you. This is what you must do:

● Account for survivors and separate the living from the dead. Carry out first aid as necessary (see Survival First Aid, page 255). Start with the most serious life-threatening injuries first and work down to the minor breaks, cuts and bruises.
● Search for clothing and equipment that may be useful for survival and salvage anything you can.
● Find or construct a form of shelter appropriate to your environment.
● Collect materials for making fire. Make a fire.
● Take as much food and water as appropriate, according to the available supplies. Remember not to eat too much if you have little water.
● Rest and reserve your strength. Do not move unless it is essential.

The order you do this in will depend greatly on the environment. If you are part of a group, you can each be responsible for a task. Once you are sheltered from the elements and have warmth and sustenance, your state of mind will begin to strengthen and morale in group situations will improve.

Do not worry too much about the wider picture. Solve one problem at a time – bit by bit, you will extricate yourself from your situation.

3. YOUR SURVIVAL PLAN

Preparing a survival plan requires a calm and calculated mind. Decisions made now may determine whether you live or die, so you must gather as much information possible about your situation before making a plan.

- Try to make sure you know your exact location. Do you know the rough direction to the nearest civilization? If not, you may wish to consider a route to an area where you are more likely to be found.
- Do you have any communications equipment with you? An HF radio or satellite telephone? Means of signalling to rescue/search parties, such as flares, smoke from fires, a mirror (for signalling to aircraft)? Whistles for attracting attention?
- Draw up a detailed list of food and equipment immediately available to you. Survival is, in essence, about making the best use of available resources so that what is lacking can be made useful, and what is available can be used in the most efficient way. Try to estimate how long you can survive on what you have. How much water do you have? Is there more water nearby?
- Check your own physical condition and that of others. You may need time to deal with injuries and recover your strength.
- Assess the current weather conditions. Could a search and rescue party successfully reach you? Will you need to wait for better conditions?

The mental and physical quality that is most required of you as a survivor is endurance. It will not be easy to solve all the problems with which you are faced. Only you can decide what you can endure and how far you can push yourself.

4. CLOTHING – IT CAN SAVE YOUR LIFE

If you have just walked away from a plane crash or similar accident and find yourself in a hostile climate dressed in unsuitable everyday clothes, you will be forced to improvise. In such a case, always remember the layer principle. Several thin layers of clothing insulate the body much better than one or two thick layers. The layering system also transfers sweat away

MESS PACK AND CONTENTS

Mess tin

Tea and coffee pouches

Chocolate

Milk and sugar pouches

Chocolate candy

Rice cake

Half toothbrush

Mini shaving foam

Mini toothpaste tube

Half razor

Soap and flannel

Fluorescent survival bag

Small flashlight

from the body. Note, too, the principles involved when choosing clothing in specific regions. People wearing bright colours are much easier to see by rescue teams than people wearing camouflage or drab colours.

FROM THE SKIN OUTWARDS

Known as the 'base layer', lightweight thermal vests not only keep you warm, they can keep you cool too. Most modern thermal vests or t-shirts draw moisture away from the surface of the skin, keeping you dry and warm. In hot climates, they also aid evaporation, helping to cool the skin. Long johns of the same material make up the base layer of your system.

In recent years, single-layer insulating clothing has been developed. Although slow to be accepted, it is now the preferred clothing for a large number of outdoor specialists. The garment is made from 'Pertex' lined with fibre-pile material. Single-layer garments are worn next to the skin, so you should bear this in mind when you are buying such items. A snug, close fit means that it becomes more effective at transferring moisture away from the skin and out through the breathable Pertex into the outside air.

MID-LAYER GARMENTS AND SHIRTS

Micro-fleece shirts are excellent mid-layer garments; they have the ability to draw away moisture and should be close-fitting. Lightweight woollen shirts also work very well. Try to buy shirts and mid-layer clothing before going to shop for a jacket. Your jacket should fit comfortably over the top without restricting movement. This layer is the most effective insulating layer of the system: to function properly, it must be kept dry. In the polar regions, keeping this insulating layer dry at all times is a major problem.

PULLOVERS

When exerting yourself physically, it is unwise to wear too much clothing, otherwise you will not be left with anything warm and dry to put on when you need it. Keep a warm, dry pullover and/or fleece available to wear when, for example, you have stopped walking; make sure it is accessible in your backpack. 'Wind stopper' or 'Wind bloc' fleece jackets can be worn over a thin fleece pullover to make a more versatile combination.

Remember to allow for the thickness of your fleece clothing when you come to buy your outer jacket.

JACKETS – SHELL LAYER

Jackets come in a wide variety of materials, designs and prices. Make sure you buy one made from breathable materials, which allow body vapour to exit but prevent water from entering. Avoid waterproof materials: waterproof cagoules are fine if you are standing still, but once you start to do any form of physical exercise, your clothing soon becomes soaked from body moisture held in by the waterproof outer garment. So invest in a jacket made from a 'breathable' material. It will not be cheap, but what price do you put on your life?

Gore-tex is fashionable, but tends to be heavy and bulky to pack. Ventile cotton fabric is also excellent, as it is light and comfortable to wear. It was developed to make survival suits for aircrew during the Second World War. Once immersed in water, the fibres swell, creating a waterproof barrier. The material still looks wet, but lets little moisture through. It also dries very quickly. Look for jackets that have deep hoods with a wired peak and pockets that are rain/snow proof.

TROUSERS

Light, quick-drying and windproof – these are the qualities to look for. As long as the upper body is warm, light trousers are adequate even in cold climates. Reinforced knee covers are an advantage, as are extra pockets to carry maps, and so on. Trousers made from Terylene/cotton or gabardine-type materials are best.

WATERPROOF TROUSERS

These should fit over your trousers and be fitted with side zips to allow you to put them on without having to take your boots off. It is a good idea to choose waterproof trousers made from breathable material. The more expensive trousers are designed with articulated knees that make sitting down and walking uphill more comfortable.

BOOTS AND GAITERS

Take great care in selecting footwear. Try to buy boots that are suitable for the kind of activity you are planning and do not just go for the strongest-looking pair – make sure you take advice. Boots made for mountaineering can be made from either leather or plastic and will have semi-rigid or even totally rigid soles so that they can be fitted with crampons for ice climbing. Low-level walking boots will have flexible soles and are often made from cordura fabric.

Ideally, boots should be broken in and well adjusted to your feet before you use them in earnest. When buying boots, take the socks you will be wearing to the shop with you and try the boots on over the socks. Experienced mountaineers wear two pairs of socks, a thin pair with a thick pair over them for comfort and to prevent blistering. It is also wise to shop for boots in the afternoon when your feet are warm and expanded.

Always carry a spare pair of laces around with you and keep the uppers waterproof and supple with a generous coating of wax. Regularly check your boots for rotten stitching and other faults – remember, if you look after your boots, they will look after you.

Gaiters are also a valuable addition, keeping snow, stones, dust, sand and rain out of your boots. Gaiters that zip up the front are easier to put on.

HEADWEAR

Up to 50 per cent of your body heat can be lost through the head, so headwear is a vitally important aspect of your equipment. Make sure you have at least one good hat with you. In a cold environment, you will require something that will also keep the cold and wind off your ears and neck. If you know that you are going to be wet, check that your headgear is waterproof to supplement the hood of your jacket. In the desert, it is a good idea to follow the example of the Arabs and carry a 'keffiyeh', or Arab headdress, also known as a 'shemagh'. If you cannot obtain the real thing, carry a piece of cloth about 100cm (40in) square that can be folded to cover the head, neck and shoulders, and wrapped around the face if necessary.

5. YOUR BACKPACK

Backpacks come in countless shapes and sizes and it is important that you choose one that is the right size for your needs. The backpack you choose will depend on the amount you have to carry and the objective of your expedition. The principle of carrying a load on your back is that if it is high and close to your body, the weight will be directed down to the ground with the least amount of strain on your back and shoulders. The further the weight is behind you, the more it will pull back on the shoulders and create pain around the shoulders and neck.

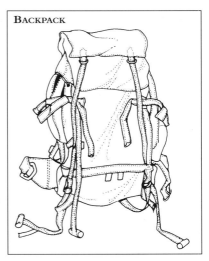

BACKPACK

Remember to pack the backpack in such a way that quick changes of clothing, such as putting on a warm sweater or a dry pair of socks, can be done without having to unpack the whole thing. Some packs are designed with brightly coloured interiors so that gear is less likely to get lost in a black hole!

Lining the pack with a polythene bag is a very good idea; this guarantees that everything in the pack remains dry. Military personnel often wrap individual items of gear in separate waterproof bags to ensure they stay dry. By doing this, the soldier can even cross a river, using his backpack as a raft, without wetting any gear.

If you intend to attach items such as an ice axe, then make sure your chosen pack has fitted straps and holders for this purpose.

6. STAY CLEAN AND DRY

Above all, remember that clean dry clothes are warm clothes. There is an old Inuit saying, 'He who sweats, dies'. In polar regions and high mountains, this is certainly true, but staying dry will extend your survival time dramatically even in temperate climates. This is why it is so important to have a clothing system that transfers body moisture away from the skin and out through the layers of clothing and at the same time stays dry. On extended expeditions, take all opportunities to wash and dry your base and mid-layer clothing. Not only will this improve the insulating qualities of your clothing, but putting on freshly washed clothes is also a great boost to your morale.

Conversely, in very hot climates there is a temptation to take off clothes that have become wet with sweat – don't! Although wet clothing is extremely uncomfortable, sweat in clothing cools the trapped air between the clothing and the skin. This results in an overall decrease in sweat gland activity and thus a reduction in water loss.

7. YOUR SURVIVAL TIN

Put together a survival kit of the most useful pieces of equipment. These are inexpensive and can fit easily into a small tin (an old tobacco tin is

SURVIVAL TIN

Windproof matches

Tin box

Candle

Flint and saw striker

Compass

Sewing kit

Water purification tablets

Heliograph

Safety pins

Fishing kit

Water bags

Potassium permanganate

Wire snare

ideal). Carry it at all times (in either your backpack or pocket) to greatly increase your chances of survival regardless of the circumstances. Once you are used to carrying the tin, you will feel lost without it. The contents should include:

- Windproof matches – but use only when other improvised fire-making methods have failed.
- Candle – tallow wax can be eaten if necessary.
- Flint and striker/small saw and metal bar. Both will easily produce sparks to light a fire. Strike the flint stone with metal or draw the saw across the bar
- Sewing kit
- Water purification tablets
- Compass
- Heliograph (or old compact disc)
- Safety pins
- Magnifying glass
- Fishing kit
- Wire saw – this can cut through thick branches quite easily and should be smeared with grease to protect it from rust.
- Water bags (large polythene bags) – large, thin-gauge polythene bags are useful for carrying water as well as for constructing solar stills and vegetation bag
- Potassium permanganate
- Snare wire – brass wire is best for animal snares, as it does not rust and can be used repeatedly.

REMEMBER!
Never carry anything that is useless. Throw away all dead weight and items that are unsuitable for the terrain you are in. Take only lightweight foods.

8. KNIVES

A strong, wooden-handled survival knife and a pocket knife with lockable blade will make life easier in a survival situation. The knife has many uses — for example, chopping wood, skinning animals, gutting fish, and opening tinned food.

Keep it clean and sharp! Use a round stone with a rough and fine grain to sharpen the knife. Make sure the stone is wet.

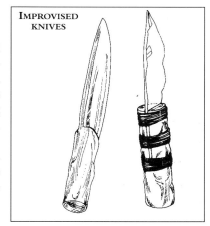

IMPROVISED KNIVES

9. VEHICLE PREPARATION AND MAINTENANCE

You will greatly reduce the danger of becoming stuck in a remote area if you have checked and maintained your vehicle properly. Make sure that you are able to carry out routine servicing or replacements in the field.

Make sure you check:

- Engine oil level
- Radiator water level
- Water in washer canisters
- Battery water level and terminals
- Power steering fluid level
- Windshield-wiper blades and jets
- Lights
- Tyre pressures and condition of tyres and wheels

For long journeys and expeditions, you will need to be confident that the following items are in working order:

ELECTRICAL

Lights, fuse boxes, spark plugs, distributor cap and rotor arm, condenser, starter motor and alternator.

BODY AND FITTINGS

Springs, shock absorbers, chassis and engine/gearbox mounts, half-shafts, differentials, brake drums, brake callipers, brake pads/shoes, clutch, radiator, water hoses, thermostat, water pump.

OIL, LUBRICANTS AND FILTERS

Filters for oil, fuel and air, brake and clutch fluids, oil for engine, gearbox, transfer box, differentials and hubs.

ADDITIONAL EQUIPMENT

New and spare tyres (adapted to the environment), lights, batteries, lockable boxes and padlocks, additional fuel tank, roof rack with jerry can holders if necessary, and engine snorkel.

TOOLS

Wrenches/spanners, hammer, feeler gauge, grease gun, pump, spare nuts and bolts, hose clips, tape, torque wrench, puncture repair kit, jump leads, tool roll, ratchet set with spark plugs, axle stands with off-road pads, tyre levers, valve tool and spare valves and exhaust repair gum.

SPARES

You will need to gauge the likely availability of spares for the particular make of vehicle in the region you will be driving in. Check the dealer network. You are likely to need spares for the following:

Brake and indicator lights, inner tubes, alternator, headlamp, radiator sealant and flush, shock absorbers, power-steering fluid, engine oil, fan belts, thermostat, wheel bearings, gaskets, wing mirror, brake shoes/pads, water hoses.

VEHICLE RECOVERY

The following may be required if your vehicle is stuck in mud, ice or sand:

Winch, large bow and D-shackles, tow-rope, kinetic recovery rope, high-lift jack with jacking plate, spade.

VEHICLE PROTECTION

Depending on the kind of terrain you will be negotiating, you may need some or all of the following:

Bull bars, sump guard, sand channels, armoured brake hoses, light covers, roll cage.

10. HOW TO DRIVE OFF-ROAD

In general, you will want to keep the vehicle moving and have maximum traction. Do not drive too fast off-road and try not to come to a halt in a soft area, such as mud or sand, which will cause wheel spin.

GETTING STUCK

If you do come to a halt and the wheels start spinning, take your foot off the accelerator immediately and plan what to do next. If you keep the wheels spinning, the vehicle will simply dig deeper into the hole. If stuck in a soft area, first try reversing out slowly. If the vehicle still does not move, rock gently in a forward gear to try to tease it out of the hole.

If this does not work, get out of the vehicle and consider whether it will be possible to place brushwood or stones under the wheels to improve traction. You may have the option of either towing the vehicle out with another vehicle, or using a winch with one end attached to the front of your vehicle and the other to a solid object, such as a tree.

When towing or winching, follow these guidelines:

- Keep bystanders well clear of the length of the towing cable.
- If you are in the vehicle, raise the bonnet for protection.
- Wear strong gloves when handling the cable.
- Wear boots with good grip so that you do not slip.
- Put a piece of canvas on the middle of the cable to reduce recoil.
- Place the winch sling low round a tree or rock.

RUTS

Drive across ruts at a diagonal in order to keep all four wheels on the ground and to provide the maximum traction. If the ruts are not too deep, you can drive along them rather like a train. Take care of sudden spins on the wheel and try not to fight the direction of the ruts. If they are too deep, you will need to place one side of the wheels on the top of one of the ruts and the other side of the wheels on the verge. Take care not to slip off these two supports.

SAND

Sand becomes progressively more difficult to drive on as it becomes drier during the day. The tyres can be deflated to a pressure of about 5kg (11 lbs) per square inch to aid sand travel, but remember that this also reduces ground clearance. If the vehicle enters soft sand, change to four-wheel drive and keep the vehicle moving evenly, changing down smoothly when necessary, and keeping the wheels as straight as possible.

WATER

To drive through water, you will need to check the vehicle is waterproofed in the vital areas, such as the electrics. Wade across the water obstacle with ropes attached and carefully check the depth of the water, the strength of the current and for any hidden obstacles. You will need to ensure that any loose items either in or on the vehicle are securely lashed down.

The crossing should be performed at a low and constant speed until the vehicle is well clear of the water. Check over the vehicle and remember that there will be a temporary reduction in braking efficiency for a while after leaving the water.

HILLS

A four-wheel-drive vehicle is normally high-sided and therefore relatively easy to tip over. Hills should be negotiated straight up or down in the appropriate gear for the steepness of slope. Stay in the same gear and keep the momentum up when ascending. If you have to retreat, hold the vehicle on the brake and select reverse gear. Come down the slope backwards in reverse gear. When descending, keep the vehicle under engine braking power and do not suddenly apply the brakes, which could cause the vehicle to skid.

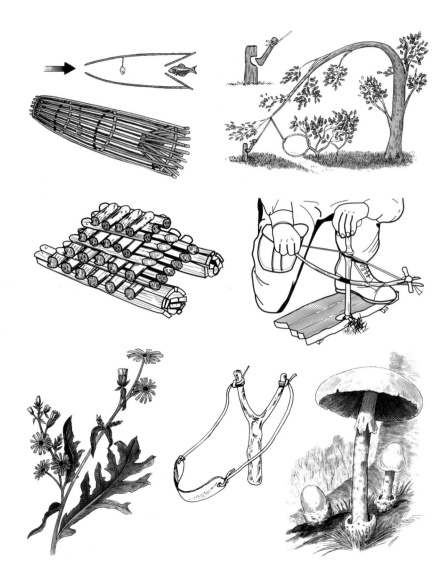

SUSTAINING LIFE

The essentials of life are few and simple. However, providing these vital essentials of life for yourself and your fellow survivors, will demand a certain amount of skilled knowledge combined with an understanding of the environment and a great deal of patience and self discipline.

Water, shelter, heat and food are basic needs to sustain life. The order in which you should search for these essentials depends on the kind of terrain you find yourself in. In hot climates, finding water followed by shelter may become you priorities. In the polar regions it would probably be shelter followed by heat of some kind.

11. WATER – A NECESSITY

Without water, there is no life. In remote wild places, you must know how to find water. Of all the elements of survival, this is the most important.

The human body is continuously losing water, even if you are doing very little physical activity. You need to replace this, otherwise you will become dehydrated and will die within a few days. Once you have assessed your survival situation, you must make finding water the number one priority. Your body loses fluids through the following:

- Urine: about 1.5 litres (2 ¾ pints) of water loss per day.
- Sweat: about 100ml (3 ½ fl oz) of water loss per day.

- Faeces: about 200ml (7fl oz) of water loss per day.
- Diffusion through the skin: about 400ml (14fl oz) of water loss per day through the cells of the skin.
- Evaporation through the lungs: when air enters the lungs, it is usually fairly dry. However, when it comes into contact with the fluids covering the respiratory surfaces, it becomes saturated with water and is then exhaled as moist air. Breathing colder air at high altitude causes a marked increase in fluid loss, and fluid loss is further increased by the extra effort required to breathe at high altitudes.

All this water loss must be replaced on a daily basis to remain healthy. To reduce water loss, rest as much as possible, preferably in a shady spot, and avoid lying down on hot or heated ground. Resist the temptation to smoke (a good reason to give up!) and do not drink alcohol, as this takes fluid from your vital organs to break it down. Both smoking and alcohol increase thirst.

Avoid too much talking, and breathe through your nose, not through your mouth. The body uses fluids to break down food, so eat as little as possible.

If you do not have access to a regular water supply, you must take all measures to minimize water loss. Keep all physical activity to a minimum. If you do need to be active, perform all the tasks slowly to reduce expenditure of energy. Rest frequently and, if possible, carry out essential work during the night or at cooler parts of the day.

In survival situations, try to resist the desire to gulp water from your bottle. Small sips taken at frequent intervals are much better.

DEALING WITH DEHYDRATION

Try to keep as warm as possible and loosen clothing to allow good blood circulation. Take water and salt gradually: one teaspoon of salt dissolved in 1 litre (1 ¾ pints) of water, then get plenty of rest.

12. YOUR WATER BOTTLE

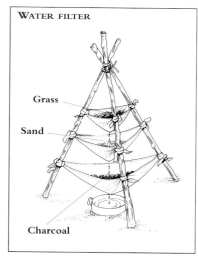

WATER FILTER

Grass

Sand

Charcoal

A good-quality water bottle should be an essential part of any back-packer's equipment. They should carry at least 1 litre (1 ¾ pints) of water and although plastic bottles are fine, an aluminium bottle has the advantage of being stronger and can be placed on a fire or stove to heat the water if necessary. In warm climates, do not put the bottle in your pack where it will be next to your back, as this will warm the water and make it less refreshing to drink. In cold climates, do not fill the bottle right to the top; you will need to allow some movement of the water to prevent it freezing. In cold climates, do keep the water bottle close to your body – your heat will also stop it from freezing.

13. WATER – WHERE TO LOOK

How to find water in specific types of terrain will be discussed in the fol-lowing chapters. However, there are several general sources of water, as well as indicators of where to look:

● Look in valleys, gulleys and watercourses. Water will normally collect at the lowest point and on the outside of a bend, so dig there.
● Look for movement of animals, birds and insects. Follow footprints and animal droppings if necessary.

- Search for any signs of greenery, especially palm trees, and keep a weather eye open for storm clouds, rain and lightning in the distance – head in that direction.
- Walk along the foot of cliffs and rock outcrops – water may have collected in the depressions or hollows in the rock. Look and listen for signs of water inside caves. Water often drips from the roof of caves and collects in pools. Look inside rock fissures for small pools of water and, if necessary, use a tube to suck the water out.
- If the water you find is brackish (slightly salty), trace the spring from where the water is coming – it may be fresher there.

14. WATER – MAKING FRESH WATER FROM SEAWATER OR URINE

As a last resort, you can produce fresh water by distilling seawater or even urine. Place a tube into the top of a sealed container filled with seawater or urine, with the other end of the tube leading to a sealed empty container. Heat the container filled with water over a fire. This will produce water vapour, which will travel along the tube then cool, filling the empty container with drinkable water.

15. FIRE – A USEFUL TOOL

Fire has long been one of the fundamental tools of mankind, offering a multitude of ways to master the environment. From neolithic times, man learned how to make fire by creating friction with tools, such as saws and drills and by producing sparks with stones such as flint.

Whichever area you find yourself in, whether it be deserts, tropics or polar regions, a fire is always essential. A fire will provide warmth and dry clothes, it will cook food and heat drinks, it will keep wild animals at bay and ward off insects. It provides light, it can be used for signalling and, last but not least, a fire is a morale booster.

In order to start and maintain a successful fire it is vital to collect the right grades of material and to get the balance right between the different elements of the fire, which are air, heat and fuel.

16. FIREMAKING MATERIALS

TINDER

This is required to get a fire started from the first sparks and may consist of wood shavings, lining of bark, sawdust, cotton fluff, bird down, dried grass or pine needles.

KINDLING

This is the material you use to expand the fire to the stage when it can take larger fuel. It includes twigs, bark, tufts of dry grass, paper or rags soaked in fuel.

FUEL

This may be wood, such as dead branches or the inside of trees, coal, peat (as long as it is dry enough – look at the top of undercut banks), dry animal dung, or dry grasses twisted into bunches.

17. FIRE – WHERE TO BUILD IT

Build the fire in a place where it will not be put out by a strong wind or falling snow, or where it is likely to set light to vegetation or your equipment. Consider whether you will need to build stones round the fire to concentrate the heat (for cooking), or whether you will need to construct a reflector to maximize the heat in a shelter.

The fire should be built on a firm base, which can be made up of stones, green wood or solid earth (this may involve digging down). The fire may need to be in a hole in the ground or surrounded by rocks if wind is likely to be a problem.

18. TYPES OF FIRES

There are a number of different fire lays, which are suitable for different uses and areas.

SAFETY NIGHT FIRE

This type of fire is designed to burn through the night with minimal risk of falling logs. It can also include a heat reflector, set back from the fire. It is designed to have few air spaces, so that the flame will burn low, and two leaning logs have the effect of pushing the fire away from your shelter.

LONG FIRE

This fire can be constructed either as a trench or between two parallel

LONG FIRE

green logs. The logs should be thick, and may be supported by two sticks to improve the airflow.

T-FIRE

Just as it sounds, this is a fire kindled in a simple T shape carved out in the earth. It is an ideal fire lay for cooking on, since the main fire can be maintained in the top part of the T, while cooking can be done on hot coals and embers that fall into the stem of the T.

TEPEE FIRE

This fire is good for both cooking and heat, and is constructed with a slanting stick fixed into the ground over some tinder. Other sticks are then leant on the slanting stick, leaving a suitable opening on the wind side. The fire should be lit with your back to the wind.

TEPEE FIRE

STAR FIRE

This is an economical fire, which should be made with hardwood logs. The logs are arranged in a star shape and gradually pushed inwards as they burn away.

PYRAMID FIRE

Lay two logs parallel to each other, and lay a number of smaller logs across them to form a base. Lay another layer of yet smaller logs at right angles to form the next layer, and so on, until you have a small layer at the top on which to light your tinder. The fire will gradually burn downwards, making it a good long-term fire to have during the night.

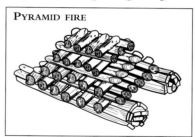

PYRAMID FIRE

19. LIGHTING A FIRE

Make sure you gather all materials before you start.

MATCHES

Windproof matches are the easiest and most obvious way of lighting a fire, and you should have a set in your survival tin. You might, however, wish to keep these for emergencies or you may have run out. If you are planning to set out on a journey, keep the matches, since you will have less time when travelling to set up other means of fire-lighting.

MAGNIFYING GLASS

Again, you should carry a magnifying glass in your survival tin, and its advantage over matches is that it will not wear out. Angle the glass to obtain a concentrated ray of heat on to some dry tinder, which should start smoking and then glow red. Blow gently to encourage a flame.

FLINT

In your survival tin, you should have at least one fire-lighting piece of equipment. Strike a piece of flint stone with metal to produce a strong spark. Otherwise, draw the saw across the bar for the same effect.

BATTERY

You can attach wires to each terminal of the battery and touch the wires together to produce a spark. Wire wool burns very well when placed across battery terminals.

GUNPOWDER

You can carefully remove a bullet from a round and use its gunpowder to start a fire.

BOW AND DRILL

This is one of the oldest methods of starting a fire. Used for thousands of years, it is a very effective way of starting a fire, but requires patience and lots of practice.

HAND DRILL

This is a similar method to the bow and drill, but without the bow. Rub a piece of hollow softwood between your hands, running them down the

BOW AND DRILL

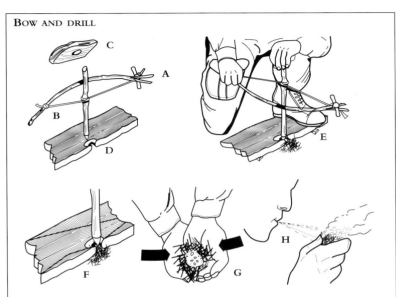

Make the bow from a piece of willow with a string stretched across it, end to end (A). The drill should be a single shaft of dry wood with one end pointed and the other rounded (B). The rounded end should fit into a hole hollowed out of a fist-sized piece of wood (C), which is used to hold the drill vertical in the hand. The pointed end goes downwards into a notch in a piece of wood, below which is tinder (D). Move the bow in a regular way back and forth so that the string turns the drill (E). With increasing pressure and speed, it creates the friction in the lower block of wood that will eventually produce smoke and light the tinder (F). Remove the bow and spindle and place the tinder next to the glowing ember (G). Roll tinder around the burning ember and blow to burn the tinder (H).

FIRE PLOUGH

Hardwood

Softwood

shaft as you go. The effect will be similar to that described above.

FIRE PLOUGH

Cut a groove into a softwood base and then use a hardwood stick to plough up and down it. Small particles of wood are thrown up by the ploughing and the friction should eventually ignite them.

20. TOOLS AND WEAPONS

If you are a serviceman, you may be armed with a rifle or pistol, which will provide security and be an advantage when hunting game. If you are a civilian, you will obviously be limited by the hunting and weapon-carrying laws and regulations of the country you are visiting. Never try to enter a country without declaring a weapon. You can carry something light such as a catapult that can be kept with your survival pack.

CLUB

The club is a basic and useful tool. It can be used for finishing off animals caught in traps, or for killing slow-moving animals, and also provides a sense of security.

The easiest club to make is a medium-sized staff that is thick at one end and fits securely into the hand. You may find a piece of wood that fits the requirement; otherwise, you can fashion one with your knife.

Other types of club can be made in the stone-age manner. Take a forked stick and fit a slightly narrower stone into the fork, and lash the fork ends securely. Alternatively, the end of the wood can be shaved and bent over the stone, to be lashed back onto the shaft. This kind of club will require careful construction and maintenance.

THROWING STICK

Find a piece of hardwood bent naturally at about 45° and shape it like a boomerang. If you cannot find a curved stick, use a straight one about 60cm (2ft) long with a thickened end.

SPEAR

The simplest kind of spear is a bamboo shaft shaved on one side at the end. This will provide a very sharp and useful weapon that can be used on small game. Similar spears can be made from hardwood poles sharpened at the end. Alternatively, attach a piece of sharp metal or bone to the end of a shaft by splitting the shaft at the end and inserting the blade into the groove before lashing it securely.

A pronglike effect can also be achieved by splitting the end of the shaft and keeping the sharp points apart with spacers lashed in. This kind of spear will be useful for fishing.

BOW AND ARROW

This classic hunting equipment should be constructed with some care, and with the knowledge that it will have a limited lifespan since you will not be using seasoned wood. Try to use a hardwood stick and fashion it in such a way that it is evenly weighted at both ends, taking advantage of any natural bend in the wood.

A stick can be shaved on the insides at both ends (away from the central area, which will be gripped in the hand), in order to improve its qualities. Cut notches at both ends for the string, which should ideally be made from rawhide. Sling the bow taut but not too tight.

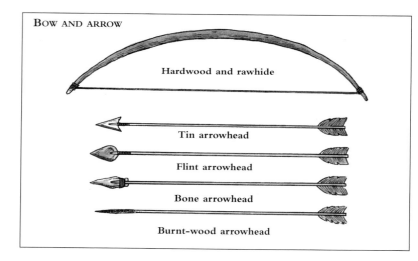

BOW AND ARROW

Hardwood and rawhide

Tin arrowhead

Flint arrowhead

Bone arrowhead

Burnt-wood arrowhead

The wood can be maintained by rubbing animal fat or oil into it. The arrows can be sharpened hardwood sticks or have suitable pieces of stone, bone, metal or glass attached. Ideally, the arrows should have feathers to improve the flight, but it is not strictly necessary. Make a notch at the end of the arrow to fit into the bowstring.

CATAPULT

You will need a Y-shaped stick as well as some elastic material, such as the inner tube of a tyre.

SLING

One piece of material will hold one or more stones. The sling is swung in the direction of the prey and one end of the material is released. Practice will be required to achieve accuracy.

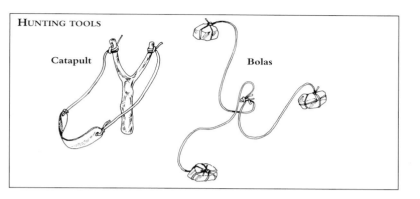

HUNTING TOOLS

Catapult

Bolas

BOLAS

The traditional weapon of the South American gauchos, the bolas consists of stones attached to string about 1m (3ft) in length. Three stones should be enough. Swing the stones above your head, taking care not to hit yourself, and release in the direction of the prey. Practice is definitely required if this weapon is not to be of greater danger to yourself than to your prey.

FISHHOOKS

You can make fishhooks out of any small pieces of sharp material that are likely to be swallowed by a fish when it takes the bait. A gorge can be made out of a small piece of hardwood, notched in the middle to take the line, and sharp at both ends.

21. TRAPPING ANIMALS

There is food available in nature's pantry, but obtaining it can require both hard work and skill. You need to be aware also of the dangers presented by certain kinds of animals.

It is important to have a good idea of the size of the animal you wish to trap, as well as to find out where its runs and trails are. This can be determined by looking for droppings, tracks, burrows, hair and fur.

The difference between an animal trail and a run is that the trail will be used by a variety of animals, whereas the run is used by only one species. Make sure that your trap is adapted to the run and to the animal you wish to catch.

If you are going to stalk animals, make sure you have not used any strong soaps or other scent, and wash yourself in clean water to remove other smells. You can help to mask your smell by standing in the smoke of a fire for a while.

When hunting, move against the wind and start out at first light. Do not take long strides, but remain balanced. Move carefully, rolling the foot from the heel through to the toes on each step, so that you can feel for breakable twigs, and other things likely to make a noise, under your feet. Get down and crawl on your hands and knees when necessary to avoid being seen by alert animals. Stop moving when an animal looks in your direction. Move again when it resumes feeding.

When you get within range, aim at a point just behind the front shoulder. This is the area on an animal where you have the best chance of hitting the heart and killing it swiftly.

If you find yourself confronted by a dangerous animal, breathe deeply to control your nerves and to convey confidence to the animal. Talk calmly and move away slowly and with assurance.

22. BUILDING 'DEADFALL' TRAPS

Deadfalls are activated either by trip wires or by bait. If the animal runs through a wire or takes the bait, a weight such as a heavy log, branch or stone falls on it and traps or kills it.

REMEMBER!

Deadfall traps are easily set off and can kill humans. Always remember where you have set your traps.

MAKING A FIGURE FOUR TRIGGER

A figure four trigger consists of an upright stick, a release stick and a bait stick.

For the upright stick, cut the top at an angle and square off the tip to allow it to fit into a notch in the release stick. Cut a square notch near the bottom to fit a corresponding square notch in the bait stick. Flatten the sides of the stick at this notch to guarantee a good fit.

For the release stick, cut the top so the deadfall will rest on it securely until triggered. Cut a notch near the top in which to fit the upright stick. Then, cut the bottom end at an angle to fit into the bait stick.

To make the bait stick, cut a notch near one end in which to place the end of the release stick. Shape the other end to hold the bait and cut a square notch at the spot where it crosses the upright stick. The notches in the upright stick and the bait should fit firmly together.

GREENLANDIC FOX TRAP

Rest the trigger on a stone or a piece of wood to stop it sinking into the ground.

BIRD TRAP
A bird trap can consist simply of nooses suspended over a branch where birds alight.

Do not tackle animals such as bears, wolves, big cats, crocodiles, alligators and poisonous snakes, unless you feel it is absolutely necessary. Do not put yourself in a position where you are cornering a dangerous animal by blocking its escape route. Beware all animals that are still alive in traps. They will fight for their lives and deliver severe bites. All animal bites are dangerous because the bacterial presence in teeth makes it very likely that a wound will become seriously infected. (Some of the most dangerous bites in this regard are those of primates, including humans).

Make sure a large animal is dead before getting too close.

23. SNARES

A snare is a wire or string loop placed in such a way that an animal is forced to put its head through it. The snare then tightens, killing the animal, though not always immediately. Commercial snares are often self-locking, but the homemade variety can be just as effective. You should have some snare wire in your survival tin. Try to disguise your human smell on the snare by smearing your hand with mud when handling it, and/or covering the snare with ashes.

TWITCH-UP SNARE
This type of snare will release a branch under tension or with a counter-weight. Use two forked sticks, one with a short fork to act as a catch. One stick is driven into the ground, while the other is attached to cord hold-

ing a sapling under tension. This device should be set up in such a way that when the animal runs through the snare, it pulls the fork attached to the sapling away from the catch.

An alternative method is to set two sticks with notches in them into the ground on either side of the animal's run. Set a crossbar into the notches. Attach one end of a cord to the sapling and tie the other end to the crossbar. The crossbar should be high enough not to impede the run of the animal, and the open snare should be set below it.

24. SNARES – WHERE TO POSITION THEM

Position the snare in the animal's run in such a way that it will be difficult

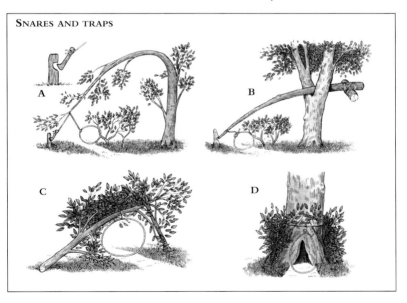

SNARES AND TRAPS

A

B

C

D

for it to avoid. Keep the loop open and unrestricted, and a proper distance off the ground. Wire snares are easy to position because of their rigidity.

Set snares on heavily used trails or in areas where animals feed on vegetation or a carcass (see page 45: A, B and C), or near a den or frequently visited food store (D). Do not place the snare too near water, as the animal will be extra alert in these areas. Arrange the surrounding vegetation in such a way that there is a tunnel just before the snare, slightly wider than the animal's body. Take care to avoid breaking vegetation when setting up the channel and leave the area looking as natural as possible, by, for example, smearing mud into cuts in trees.

The snare must be attached to a firmly embedded stick or branch that will hold the animal when it struggles. Make sure you regularly check any snares you have set up, since the animal will have a better chance of escaping given more time, and it may also be taken by another predator. Animals will normally be moving about at first and last lights.

25. GUTTING ANIMALS

When an animal is caught, it must be gutted and skinned properly to prevent it causing unpleasant side effects when eaten.

- First drain the blood by slitting the throat.
- Cut around the anus and cut the skin parallel to the penis if the animal is male (A).
- Insert two fingers between the skin and the membrane containing the entrails. Place the knife blade between your two fingers and cut up towards the chin (B).
- Cut the diaphragm at the rib cage, and cut the pelvic bone and remove the anus (C).
- Split open the breast and remove as much of the windpipe as possible (D).

GUTTING ANIMALS

- Turn the animal on its side and roll out the entrails (E). It is sometimes easier to do this after the animal has been skinned.

If it is a large animal, you will need to cut it up to make it manageable. You can cut through the tissue connecting the front legs to the body and cut off the hindquarters. Cut away the muscles on either side of the spine and separate the ribs from the backbone. You can either cook large pieces of meat over a spit or boil them. Boil or stew smaller pieces.

26. SKINNING ANIMALS

It is easier to skin an animal immediately after killing, and it may be easier to remove the entrails after it has been skinned.

Slit the skin from anus to neck, taking care to cut round the anus. Cut up the inside of the leg to the knee joint. Cut round the legs at the joint. Beginning at the rear legs, peel the skin away until you reach the back, and then remove the skin downwards towards the head.

CURING
A rough way of curing the skin is to wash it to remove blood and fleas and scrape the inner side of the skin using a stone and sand or earth.

BIRDS
Remove feathers by plucking or skinning. Open up the body and remove entrails, except the craw, heart and liver. Cut off the feet.

27. FISHING

Fish are an excellent source of protein and can be caught in a variety of ways. Fish tend to be attracted to the shaded parts of streams and to deep pools and backwaters.

BAIT

The bait that you use should be as similar as possible to what the fish in the area are already feeding on – for example, worms, insects, minnows, maggots or scraps of flesh.

FISH TRAPS

You can construct traps, such as fish baskets, made of several sticks lashed together to form a funnel pointing into the basket with a bait. The fish should be able to swim in but not out again.

A similar trap can be made out of a bottle. Cut a plastic bottle off at the head, then turn the head round and insert it into the bottle. To use a glass bottle, make sure the bottom of the bottle is broken and jagged.

LINE FISHING

You can leave lines out in a river with weights attached and smaller lines trailing off them. This gives you a better chance of getting a catch. Check the lines for a catch regularly, but not frequently.

FLY FISHING

A fishing rod can be improvised from a suitable branch with a line and fly attached. The fly should be whisked on to the surface of the water upstream and allowed to float downstream. Fish will attempt a bite only during seasons when flies and insects are at large. You can use something like a beetle or grasshopper for this kind of fishing, as it will struggle on the surface of the water and attract the attention of fish.

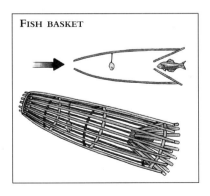

FISH BASKET

NETS

You can narrow a stream with stones in order to channel fish to where a net is placed. Ensure the net is held securely so that it is not taken away by the fish or any other floating material. Nets can be strung out across a stream with stones to weigh down the bottom of the net.

SPEARFISHING

You will need to be near shallow water where the fish are large and plentiful. You can use a piece of sharpened bamboo or sapling as a spear, or use a pole with a knife, or other blade, attached to the end.

Put the end of your spear under water and move it slowly towards the fish. Then impale a fish with a sharp strike. If you are successful, it is probably best not to try and lift the fish onto the bank with the spear, but to reach down and grab the fish with your free hand.

28. CLEANING A FISH

Slit from the anus to behind the gills and pull out the internal organs. Wash and clean the flesh and cut off the fins and tail. Cut down to the spine, but not through it. Cut round the spine, finishing behind the gills on both sides. Insert your thumb along the top of the spine and pull it away from the flesh. The ribs should come away with the spine.

29. COOKING METHODS

BOILING

Ideally, you should use a metal container, such as a can, but you can also boil water in a bamboo stem if it is slanted over the fire.

ROASTING

The meat should be skewered on a spit and turned over hot embers.

Ensure the meat does not cook too quickly on the outside without cooking the inside.

BAKING
You can either use some form of metal container as an oven or improvise by digging a pit under a fire.

FRYING
Place food on a flat piece of rock on a fire.

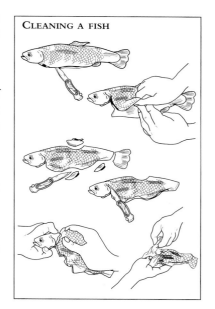

CLEANING A FISH

- *Insects and worms*
  Boil, or dry and crush before adding to soups and stews.
- *Shellfish*
  Boil as soon as possible to prevent them going off and to destroy harmful organisms.
- *Turtles and tortoises*
  Boil until the shell comes off. Cut meat and cook.
- *Reptiles*
  Gut and cook in their skins in hot embers. When the skin splits, remove and boil. Cut off snake heads before cooking. Skin frogs and roast on a stick.
- *Birds*
  Boil all carrion. Roast young birds.
- *Fish*
  Stew or wrap in leaves and bake.

● *Meat*
Cut into cubes and boil. Wild pig is infested with worms and liver fluke. Venison can also contain worms.

30. SURVIVING ON PLANTS

In general, you should avoid:
● Any fruit that is overripe or showing any signs of mildew or fungus.
● Weeds, leaves or seeds with an almond-like scent, which is an indication of cyanide compound.
● All mushrooms unless you are 100 per cent certain they're safe (see Tips 32 and 33).
● Plants with a three-leaved growth pattern.
● Beans, bulbs or seeds from pods.
● Foliage that looks like parsley, dill, carrot or parsnip.
● Grain heads with pink, purplish or black spurs.

THE 'UNIVERSAL EDIBILITY TEST'
Use this when in doubt. But remember, this test does not apply to fungi/mushrooms.

● Test one part of the plant at a time. Separate the plant into parts – leaf, flower, bud, stem, root. Smell the plant for acid.
● Fast for at least eight hours before testing the plant. During the fast, test for contact poisoning on your elbow or wrist.
● Do not take anything other than water and the tested plant into the mouth during testing. Choose a small amount of the plant and prepare it in the way you want to eat it. Touch a small portion on the outside of your lip to test for a burning sensation or itching. Wait three minutes.
● If there is no reaction, place the plant on your tongue and wait for 15 minutes.

- If there is still no reaction, thoroughly chew a pinch (without swallowing) and again leave for 15 minutes. If you sense no burning, itching or numbing sensations, swallow the food.
- Wait for eight hours. If there are any ill effects, induce vomiting (put two fingers down the back of the throat) and drink plenty of water. If you suffer no ill effects, eat a quarter of a cup of the same plant prepared in the same way.
- Wait another eight hours, and if all is well, the plant, as prepared, is safe for eating.

REMEMBER!

One part of a plant may be edible and other parts may not be. If it is edible cooked, it may not be edible raw – before eating it raw, re-do the test. Different individuals may react in different ways to the same plant.

EDIBLE PLANTS TO LOOK FOR

For specific regions, you can find lists of edible plants in the relevant chapter. The following list is restricted to examples of plants that do not fall clearly into the desert, tropical or polar categories.

ALMOND

The almond can be found widely across tropical, temperate and arid areas. Similar to the peach tree, the almond is covered by a thick, brown, dry skin. Like all nuts, it is highly nutritious.

ARROWROOT

Found in moist areas throughout temperate and tropical zones. It has arrow-shaped leaves. The roots can be boiled as a vegetable.

ASPARAGUS

Found in temperate areas worldwide. In spring, green, finger-like growths accompany fine foliage and red berries. Boil young stems for at least 15 minutes before eating.

BEECH
Found in many temperate zones in moist areas. The tree has a light grey bark and dark green leaves. Beechnuts are edible after removing a thin shell.

BLACKBERRY AND RASPBERRY
Found throughout temperate regions. They have prickly stems and edible fruits of different colours. The leaves can be boiled to make tea.

ARROWROOT

BURDOCK
Found widely in northern temperate zones. It has arrow-shaped leaves and pink flowers with bristly burrs. The leaf stalks can be eaten raw or cooked, and the roots boiled.

CAROB
Found in the Mediterranean, Middle East and North Africa. The seedpods are known as St John's bread. The young pods are edible either raw or boiled. Older pods can be crushed to make a porridge.

CHESTNUT
Found in temperate and tropical zones. Chestnuts are traditionally roasted in embers, which causes the shell to crack, revealing the delicious and nutritious nut.

CHICORY
Can be found in Africa, Asia, Europe and North America. The leaves are like dandelion, the flowers are light blue, and it has a tall stem that can

reach almost 2m (6 ½ft). The leaves and roots can be eaten, the latter boiled.

CHUFA
Found in many parts of the world in moist areas. The leaves are similar to grass. You can boil or bake the tubers.

COMMON JUJUBE
Found widely in tropical, sub-tropical, arid and temperate regions. The fruit can be dried, and the pulp produces water.

CRAB APPLE
Found widely in the northern hemisphere and in savannas. The trees can be 1–12m (3–40ft), and have beautiful white and pink blossoms. The wild fruit itself is much smaller than the cultivated apple, and is an excellent survival staple. It can be eaten raw or boiled, or dried and stored.

CRANBERRY
Found in the cooler parts of the northern hemisphere. It is a ground creeper with red berries. It should be cooked and eaten with added sugar to avoid an astringent taste.

DANDELION
Found in open areas in the northern hemisphere. The flower grows close to the ground and has jagged leaves with bright yellow flowers. All parts of the plant are edible. The roots can be boiled and eaten as a vegetable, or roasted and ground as a coffee substitute.

CHICORY

ELDERBERRY
Found in Europe and North America, mostly in moist areas. It has large compound leaves, clusters of cream-

coloured flowers and black berries. Some versions have red berries. The fruits are edible, though take care with the rest of the plant, as it produces a strong laxative effect.

HAZELNUT
Found in Europe, North America and Asia, mostly in open areas. The bush has bristly husks round the nut which is good to eat, especially in autumn.

JUNIPER
Found in Europe, North America, Asia and North Africa. An evergreen tree, it has needle-like leaves and bluish cones. The berries can be eaten raw or the seeds roasted to make a coffee substitute.

LOTUS
Yellow-flowered lotus found in North America, and pink-flowered lotus in the Far East and many other parts of the world. The plant is edible either raw or cooked.

NETTLE
Ubiquitous plant with furry bristles that cause a sting lasting a few minutes. The nettle can be boiled for around 15 minutes and is nutritious. You can also make nettle tea. The sting from the Australian variety of nettle can be very severe, so beware!

OAK
Found in Europe, North and Central America and Asia. It can be either deciduous or evergreen. Tan oaks produce very bitter acorns, which need days to soak. Otherwise acorns can be boiled.

PERSIMMON
Found in the Far East, Africa and North America. A deciduous tree with

oblong leaves, it produces a large berry about the size of an apricot and is extremely astringent until very ripe, when it becomes sweet and palatable.

PINE
Found widely in Europe, Central and South America, North Africa, the Middle East and parts of Asia. It has needle–like leaves and a sticky sap. The pine nuts can be taken out of the cones and shelled to produce tasty soft white nuts.

REED
Found in temperate regions mostly in wet areas. The tall, coarse grass can be eaten raw or cooked.

SASSAFRAS
Found in northern temperate regions, growing to a height of up to 15m (45ft). It has deciduous leaves and soft yellow wood. You can eat the young twigs and leaves.

SEA ORACH
Found mostly in salty areas in the Mediterranean and North Africa. It has small grey leaves and flowers collected in narrow spikes. The leaves can be eaten.

SORGHUM
Found widely in warmer areas. Grass that looks like corn and which can grow up to 3m (12ft) tall. It produces seeds on its panicles, or terminal heads. The grains can be eaten any time and provide nutritious food.

TAMARIND
Found widely in Africa, Asia and tropical Central and South America. A large tree may grow to be 24m (80ft) tall. It has pale yellow flowers and a

tapering fruit consisting of a pod with seeds. Cook the seeds before eating. The pulp round the seeds **TAMARIND** can be sucked for water or used to make a drink by adding it to water, though you should probably add a sweetener like honey.

WILD DOCK AND WILD SORREL

Found widely in many zones. They are stout plants with small flowers collected in clusters. Eat the leaves either raw or cooked.

WILD ROSE

Found widely in the northern hemisphere. It is a prickly shrub with red, pink or yellow flowers. You can eat the rose hips when the petals fall. Do not eat the seeds.

31. POISONOUS PLANTS

DEATH CAMAS

Deadly poisonous. Found in the United States and eastern Siberia. It has an onion-like appearance, but not the familiar smell (which is how it can be distinguished).

OLEANDER

Found in Mediterranean and in tropical and temperate regions. Its leaves are leathery and the flowers can range from white to pink, purple or yellow. The sap is highly toxic and is used to make rat poison.

POISON IVY, POISON OAK, POISON SUMAC

Found throughout the United States and southern Canada. The appearance can vary between shiny and dull-coloured leaves. Leaflets are grouped in threes, and small yellowish or white berries are produced in summer. Its distinguishing characteristics include the regular grouping of three leaflets in each leaf, and stiff clusters of small, yellowish or white berries that appear in summer and autumn. It will cause serious contact dermatitis and severe skin rashes. Keep clear.

RENGHAS TREE
Found in India and Southeast Asia. It has alternating leaves and flowers similar to those of the poison ivy, and again will cause contact dermatitis.

FUNGI
Do not eat a mushroom unless it can be positively identified as 100 per cent safe (see Tips 32 and 33).

DEATH CAMAS

32. EDIBLE FUNGI

If you know what to look for, fungi can provide delicious survival food. Eat only fungi that you are certain are edible. If you are at all in doubt, leave it alone.

CHANTERELLE
Found in coniferous and hardwood forests in midsummer. It has an irregular lobed orange or yellow cap and has a faint smell of apricots.

GIANT PUFFBALLS
Grow in grass and shady places from late summer through to autumn. They do not have the usual gills and pores of mushrooms, and are creamy white, turning brown with age, when they become unsuitable to eat. Do not eat if the puffball is brown or purplish inside.

GIANT PUFFBALLS

TRUE MORELS

KING BOLETUS
Found in deciduous woods in summer and early autumn. The cap varies from yellow to greenish as the mushroom gets older.

OYSTER MUSHROOM
Grows on rotting tree trunks from midsummer to late autumn. Olive-coloured cap when young, fading with age.

SULPHUR MUSHROOM
Appears in the form of a brown wood rot on decaying trees and stumps.

It produces bright orange and yellow growths from summer through to autumn. Eat it only when fresh and young.

SHAGGY MANE
Found widely from spring through to autumn. It has a cylindrical cap covered with shaggy brown scales. Take care of related species that can cause poisoning.

TRUE MORELS
Found in spring in such places as orchards. The ribbed and pitted cap is greenish yellow or dark olive. Note that there are false morels, which should not be eaten.

TRUFFLES
Found underground in areas of Europe. They are whitish when young, becoming darker with age.

33. POISONOUS FUNGI

Potentially poisonous mushrooms number at least 200, and to list them all is beyond the scope of this book. Most of them have sinister names. Follow the principle that if you cannot make a positive identification, do not take the risk. A cuplike volva or stem base is a reliable sign of a poisonous mushroom, as are rings round the stem.

AMANITA FAMILY
Deadly poisonous. These mushrooms contain organic toxins that attack the central nervous system, liver, kidneys and blood vessels. Symptoms may present themselves as much as 12 hours or more after eating the mushroom. Death can follow two or three days later.

Found largely in woods and by the roadside from early summer until late autumn. They have a brightly coloured scaly cap, which can be shades of yellow or orange-yellow. The flesh is yellow beneath the skin, though white deeper down. Gills are white or pale yellow. The stem is white and scaly, and has a characteristic swelling at the volva or base, which has a frill-like ring at the top.

DEATH CAP
Deadly poisonous. Found in woodland from summer through to autumn. It has a greenish-olive cap, a pale stem, white gills and flesh, and a large volva or base.

DESTROYING ANGEL
Deadly poisonous. Found in woodland in summer and autumn. It is white all over with a scaly stem and large volva. It smells sweet and sickly.

JACK-O-LANTERN
Deadly poisonous, Jack-o-lantern is found at the decayed base of tree stumps and has saffron-yellow gills.

FLY AGARIC
Dangerously poisonous. Found in pine and birch woods in autumn. It is bright vermilion, fading to orange, and usually flecked with white scales.

PANTHER CAP
Deadly poisonous. Found in woodland, mostly beech. It has a brownish appearance

DESTROYING ANGEL

with a white-flecked cap and white gills. There are two or three hooplike rings at the base of the stem.

LEADEN ENTOLOMA

Deadly poisonous. Found in the summer and autumn, particularly in beech and oak woods. It has a dull white appearance and a convex cap. Gills turn from yellowish to salmon pink. It has no ring on the stem, and smells of radish and bitter almonds.

PANTHER CAP

SURVIVING IN MOUNTAINOUS REGIONS

Mountains are hostile and dangerous places. Freezing winds, snow, glaciers, mist and rain are all potential killers. A survivor must learn how to avoid being overcome by the forces of nature.

Finding yourself stranded on a high mountain for the first time can be a chilling experience, as this is normally an environment only frequented by experienced and well-equipped mountaineers. Mountains can kill you very quickly and each year many experienced mountaineers lose their lives. Most accidents happen when descending mountains, when tiredness takes over and basic safety rules are forgotten.

If you have survived the initial reason for being stranded in the mountains, don't allow yourself to become lost through a simple lack of concentration.

SURVIVAL IN MOUNTAINS

Although some do stand on their own, mountains usually exist in ranges. A range can be made up of either a single ridge or a series of ridges, peaks and inter-mountain ranges. Closely related ridges are called mountain systems, and more than one system joined together is called a mountain chain. A mixture of ranges, systems and chains is called a belt or cordillera.

SURVIVING IN MOUNTAINOUS REGIONS

Mountain regions can be spectacularly beautiful as well as inhospitable. They offer little protection from low temperatures and high winds. The first rule of mountain survival, therefore, is to find a way of descending as safely as possible. The following tips describe some of the basic skills that will help you survive and reach safety in mountainous regions.

The sheer unpredictability of the weather conditions on mountains can pose a number of threats to survival. Weather can change suddenly from pleasant sunshine to gloomy skies and driving rain or snow storms. By their sheer mass, mountains cause air currents to be uplifted and disturbed, producing long periods of bad weather. A dull, quiet day can soon turn into a blizzard or freezing rain, both of which can be extremely serious because of their ferocity and because of the chilling damp cold that they bring.

Conditions high on mountains can be fiercely arctic and therefore much more skill and energy are required to survive. Wind chill can quickly numb you unless you keep moving. Wind blows most strongly on mountain summits and ridges, its speed increasing with altitude. Strong winds drain your energy as you try to stay balanced while being buffeted, and they also have a powerful chilling effect on the body temperature (see Wind Chill – Tip 77). The wind-chill factor is nearly always present in the mountains. Even on sunny days, you must not underestimate the chilling effect of the wind. Rain tends to be more frequent and heavier in mountainous terrain and can soak you to the skin in a short space of time: be aware of the dangers of hypothermia (see Tip 76).

You can also face reduced visibility due to low cloud, driving rain, mist, whiteouts or storms, all of which cause navigation problems for the survivor. Snow makes for difficult route-finding because it obscures paths and sometimes buries cairns. It also makes movement far more dangerous; what would by a simple slip, easily checked in summer on long grass or heather, might turn into a long and potentially dangerous fall on snow in winter.

Being caught out and having to spend the night on a mountain should be avoided at all costs.

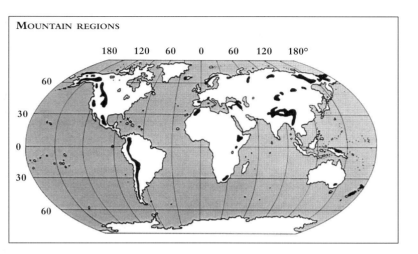

MOUNTAIN REGIONS

CLIMATE

Temperature falls at a more or less constant rate with increasing altitude – about 0.5–1°C (1°F) for every 100m (300ft). Wind systems are forced by mountains to rise and cool as they do so, causing higher precipitation on windward mountain slopes. When the wind descends the leeward slope, it warms up and precipitation reduces, creating rain shadow.

Mountains in desert regions receive little rain because the air is so dry. On equatorial mountains, where temperatures are low at high altitudes, winter and summer are indistinguishable.

Mountains in temperate regions have strongly marked seasons, being sometimes frost-free even at night in the summer, but with temperatures often below freezing in the winter.

There are also microclimate variations. Mountainsides facing the equator in temperate regions are significantly warmer than those on the opposite side.

Typically, ascending a mountain in a temperate region will involve passage through deciduous broad-leaved trees, then evergreen coniferous forest, and finally you will cross what is called the timberline (the area above which trees cannot grow) and reach an area of tundra-like dwarf shrubs and herbs. After that, vegetation can be almost non-existent.

MOUNTAIN HAZARDS

In normal circumstances, mountains and glaciers should be climbed only by experienced and properly equipped mountaineers. However, in a survival situation, you may find yourself having to negotiate mountainous terrain to get yourself out of danger and back to civilization.

ICE AXE

34. USING AN ICE AXE AND SKI-POLE

ICE-AXE

To move on snow and ice, this is a basic piece of equipment that can be used for support, braking, digging and probing. Its basic components are the head (adze and pick), a shaft and a spike. There are a huge variety of axes available, most designed specifically for technical ice climbing and of little use for general mountaineering. Look for an axe with a straight shaft around 65cm (26in) long. The axe head should have a pick with a slight curve and an adze. The adze is used for cutting steps up steep slopes and for digging out snow hole shelters in survival situations.

SKI-POLE

Telescopic ski-poles (sometimes referred to as 'trekking poles') provide a 'third leg' when traversing slopes and moving over scree and snow, and are also very useful for balance when crossing rivers. You can carry a telescopic ski-pole in a backpack.

35. AVALANCHE – UNDERSTANDING THE RISK

You should be aware of the factors that cause and effect avalanches. The more knowledge you have about avalanche conditions, the less likely you are of being an avalanche victim.

An avalanche can occur wherever snow lies, but it is influenced by certain conditions. If the snow is well bound together, the risk of avalanche is reduced. If there are marked differences in the hardness of layers of snow, the risk of avalanche increases.

Avalanches occur more frequently during winter, but also during the spring thaw. Avalanches come in many forms, from the small loose snow slides that are more of a nuisance than a danger, to the large 'slab' avalanches that sweep away trees and sometimes towns and villages.

GROUND

If the ground is hard and smooth, snow is more likely to slide over it. Long grass will also provide a slippery surface for snow.

SLOPE

If the slope is concave (curving inwards), it is less likely to have an avalanche. If it is convex (curving outwards), it is more likely to have an avalanche. Obviously, the angle of the slope is also an important factor. The steeper the slope, the more likely the snow is to slide off it. Slopes of between 20° and 50° are most likely to have an avalanche.

WIND SLAB

The most common type of avalanche is called wind slab, and is caused by the effect of wind on falling or fallen snow. Wind slab snow is chalky in appearance, has a fine texture and makes a squeaky noise when walked on. Wind slab avalanches always start with a very loud 'bang' as the snow-pack breaks away.

POWDER SNOW

Avalanches can be caused when powdery snow accumulates in conditions of no or little wind. Over 40cm (16in) of fresh snow is an indicator of a high risk of this kind of avalanche.

ICE

Avalanches caused by ice usually occur in warm weather when ice masses fall after thawing. Pinnacles of ice, or seracs, are most likely to fall in the morning or evening, due to the change in temperature.

WET SNOW

A rapid rise in temperature or an area exposed to direct sunlight indicates the risk of a wet snow avalanche. Check to see whether there are snowballs running down a hill, which is an indicator of this kind of avalanche.

CORNICE

These are overhanging masses of snow which usually form on the crests of ridges and plateaus, but which can occur at any sharp changes of angle. The most common angle of slope on which a cornice forms is 17°.

A cornice can break off well back from the actual edge, so keep as far away from the edge as possible. It is advisable to be roped up when you are negotiating a ridge with a cornice.

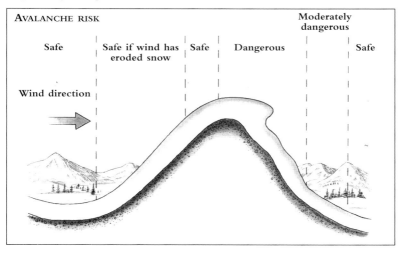

balls running down a hill, which is an indicator of this kind of avalanche.

You can assess the likelihood of an avalanche by digging a snow pit in a representative area to test the hardness. If you prod the snow with an axe shaft and notice sudden changes in resistance, that is quite a good sign that the area is prone to avalanche. You can perform the test more thoroughly by digging a snow profile, preferably all the way to the ground, which will allow you to assess differences in hardness, moisture content and crystal size in the various layers of snow. Layers of loose crystalline snow show periods of thaw. These layers will act as 'ball bearings' on which the upper snow layers can slide.

Water is a lubricant, so if the snow is very wet it will be denser and heavier, and more likely to slide. A rough guide to the wetness of snow is that if you can make a snowball out of the snow, it is quite wet. If your gloves are dripping wet from handling the snow, it is very wet.

36. AVALANCHE – WHAT TO DO IN AREAS AT RISK

Always cross a danger zone one person at a time, connected by a rope. Cross the slope as high as possible, and take advantage of any available protection, such as rock outcrops.

SWIMMING THROUGH AN AVALANCHE

If you are caught in an avalanche, do your best to maintain your present position. This may mean digging your axe into an area of snow above you that is not moving. By staying where you are, you will allow the dangerous snow to pass safely below you.

If you are falling in an avalanche, throw off your backpack (or anything else you may be carrying) and try to move across to the side of the fall by rolling sideways. Use swimming motions to try to remain near the surface. If still caught in the snow when the avalanche has stopped, use all your energy to 'swim' to the surface.

Should you find yourself buried, try to clear a breathing space in front of the face. Conserve oxygen by not shouting, which is unlikely to be heard anyway.

37. AVALANCHE RESCUE

RESCUE

Mark the spot where you saw him/her before the avalanche fell, and then the place where the avalanche hit the person. Follow the line through these two points and continue it below to find the most likely place of burial.

Call for help, but do not leave the area to find assistance that is more than 15 minutes away.

Look around the general area for personal items that may indicate where the burial site is, then systematically check the area by prob-

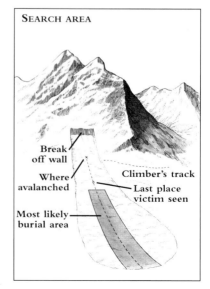

SEARCH AREA

Break off wall

Where avalanched

Climber's track

Last place victim seen

Most likely burial area

ing carefully with an axe shaft or other means.

On finding the victim, clear any snow from the mouth and airways. Remove the weight of snow from the chest. Give artificial respiration immediately if the person is not breathing, even before fully removing the victim's body from the snow.

38. GLACIERS

A glacier is a mass of ice in an area of permanent snow. The weight of snow creates a pressure that turns snow to ice, which then begins to move downhill under the force of gravity. As the glacier moves, it melts, and stops moving only when the amount that has melted is equivalent to the accumulation of snow at the source of the glacier.

The surface of the glacier is a brittle crust and this can crack under the strains of glacial movement to form features such as crevasses, ice falls or seracs, all of which constitute dangers for mountaineers.

The glacier picks up crushed rock, which is known as moraine. The rock may then be deposited in ridges along the side (lateral moraine), along the centre (medial moraine) and at the end of the glacier (terminal moraine). Moraines can be loose and dangerous to traverse.

39. NEGOTIATING GLACIERS

If possible, plan to cross a glacier in the early morning when it is still cold, before ice has turned to melt water. Take special care in areas where the glacier starts to become steeper or where it bends, as this will create dangerous features. Keep an eye out for any abnormalities in the surface of the snow, such as dark patches or dips, which may be covering a crevasse.

Take care with snow bridges (which cross crevasses), as they might give way at any moment. Always try to assess the direction of crevasses and make sure you cross them at right angles. If jumping one, remember that snow may be loose on the far side. Make sure you fall forward after the jump, preferably with an ice axe to dig in at the other side.

Temperatures may be high on the glacier during the day, but climbers should take care about how much clothing they remove because, if they fall into a crevasse, the temperature will plummet. The sun will reflect off the ice surface and burn the underside of your nose and chin. Be sure not to miss these areas when applying sun cream.

If the glacier is covered with fresh snow, features like crevasses will be difficult to see and, therefore, climbers should be roped up to each other. It is much safer to be roped up whatever the conditions.

When roped up, allow about 25m (85ft) of rope between at least two, and preferably three or more, people. Some rope can be coiled round the body, over the right shoulder and under the left arm, to make a distance between walkers of about 15m (45ft). An overhand knot should be tied round the coils and the main rope. Loose coils of rope should never be carried, and the rope should never be slack between the climbers. If the first person falls into a crevasse, the rest of the team should quickly move backwards and down on their haunches, with their heels dug into the snow to stop the fall.

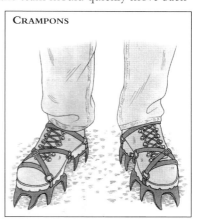

CRAMPONS

40. MOVING OVER SNOW AND ICE

You can make kick steps when walking in soft snow, but wear crampons on ice (if you have the correct kind of stiff boots).

DIRECT ASCENT

Hold the ice axe with the pick

DIAGONAL ASCENT

pointing backwards and use it for support. Move it only when both feet are fully secure in steps. Kick a step into the snow, which is angled slightly downwards. The step should be deep enough to take at least half the foot, though this may not be possible in very hard ground.

DIAGONAL ASCENT

The steps should be horizontal, created with the side of the boot, and angled slightly into the hill. Kick along the slope to saw away the snow. Push the axe into the hill with the inside hand for stability and security.

DESCENT

When coming down a mountain the steps are made with the heel of the boot, with an almost stiff leg.

Remember, take your time! Statistics prove that most accidents in mountains occur while descending.

41. ARRESTING A FALL

If you slip and you have an ice axe, immediately drive the shaft vertically into the slope and keep one hand holding it near the base. Kick both toes into the snow to get a foothold. On harder snow, use the pick of the ice axe, forcing it into the snow to create a brake.

BRAKING POSITION

One hand should be on the head of the axe and the other on the shaft. If the left hand is on the axe head, the adze should be under the left shoulder, with the right hand on the shaft to the side of the body. The pick should be forced into the slope by pushing down with the right arm and shoulder. The adze of the axe should be pushed into the hollow just below the collarbone. Pressure should be on the axe and on the knees with feet raised.

The above is the basic position, but obviously you may not be in the ideal position when you fall. The important thing is to act as quickly and instinctively as possible. This is a technique where practice will make a difference – follow the guidance of a good climbing manual.

BRAKING WITHOUT AN AXE

If you lose the axe in a fall or do not have one, use your arms, feet, hands and legs to break the fall. One technique is to roll on your front, push up

BRAKING POSITIONS

from the slope with your arms and concentrate all the pressure on your toes. This has a wedge effect, which should bring you to a halt.

42. DESCENDING FROM A MOUNTAIN

Descent is your main priority, because on a mountain you will be both cold and exposed. If you need to rest and find temporary shelter, work your way round to the lee of the mountain, out of the wind.

To make your descent easier, look out for worn paths or other signs that the route has been used by people. In poor visibility, you will need to be extremely cautious, as finding your way in a mist is difficult even for experienced climbers with compasses.

If you are scrambling down a hillside, make sure you are facing inwards towards the rock, and avoid gullies, as the risk of stone falls is greater. If you are in a group, ensure that those below are not in danger of being hit by rocks loosened by those above.

If traversing a glacier in a group, keep roped together. Follow existing tracks if possible, but be aware that they may have been left by inexperienced climbers. Beware of slopes covered with small, loose stones (scree), as they may lead to a cliff that you cannot see from the top.

DESCENTS ON SNOW AND ICE – GLISSADING

If you intend to glissade, you should be competent at ice-axe braking. Glissade only if you can see the whole slope and the area where you will stop. Glissading is a practised skill, but is really no more than a controlled slide, and loss of balance can quickly lead to an uncontrolled fall! It has often been said that there are three types of glissade – standing, sitting and involuntary – and that they often follow each other in quick succession. Glissade standing or crouching only if you have had lots of practice beforehand. In a survival situation, it is best to avoid these methods, as the chance of injury is increased. It is safer to use the sitting glissade method.

- **Standing glissade**

  Like skiing, you should adopt a relaxed position with knees slightly bent and the feet apart. Hold out the arms for balance. Turn by moving the body, and stop by turning the feet across the slope.

- **Crouching glissade**

  Crouch down grasping the ice axe, with one hand on the top and the other on the shaft. Drag the spike of the axe in the snow for balance. To brake, put your weight on the shaft of the axe.

- **Sitting glissade**

  Sit on the snow and slide down, using the axe in the same way as in the crouching glissade, one hand on the top, the other on the shaft. If you lie back and raise your feet, you will go faster. To stop, put your feet down and use the axe. Wearing waterproof trousers will keep your pants dry, but remember that you will slide a lot faster!

43. HOW TO ABSEIL

A survivor with a climbing rope can descend steep ground and vertical cliffs very quickly and with reasonable safety by 'roping down' or more commonly known as 'abseiling' or 'rappelling'. It is not an easy option, however, and is treated with caution by even the most experienced climbers. Pictures of civilians abseiling off buildings may give a false impression – they are usually under strict guidance from experienced professionals, who also act as anchormen. Resort to abseiling only if there are no options, or if you or your companions are trained in the technique.

The following description of a classic abseil assumes you are equipped with only a rope:

- First of all, find a solid anchor; a second anchor point may be used as a

ABSEILING

backup. The anchor should ideally be located above the ledge on which you are standing.

● Make sure the rope will not move once it is placed under strain. Keep the rope clear of narrow cracks in which the rope may get jammed and prevent you retrieving it when you need to. Also, keep it clear of loose rock or sharp edges that could cut into the rope, even sever it. Make sure that long hair and loose clothing do not get caught up accidentally in the ropes. If it is necessary to do a long abseil you may need to join two ropes together, in which case try a double fisherman's knot. (see Tip 46 – Mountaineering Knots)

● Tie yourself and the top of the abseil rope securely to the anchor(s). If necessary – and to avoid abseiling off the end of the rope – tie another knot in the bottom end of the abseil rope before throwing the rope down the cliff. Make absolutely sure that anyone below is aware of what you are doing, and that the rope reaches down as far as the ledge you are trying to reach.

● Pass the rope, from front to rear, between your legs, round your upper right thigh, diagonally across your chest, over your left shoulder, under your armpit and into your right hand.

● Walk slowly backwards over the edge, and crouch low if there is any danger of lifting the rope off the top of the anchor. The lower (right) hand will control the braking – you should never try to brake with the upper (left) hand. By turning your body outwards and towards your braking hand, you can make yourself more secure and also see downwards more clearly.

● When descending, go down as smoothly as possible in order to avoid a pendulum effect that may draw the rope over a sharp edge. Once you are down, beware of any rock that may be loosened by the rope as you pull it through.

REMEMBER!

The friction caused by the rope running around your body will produce a considerable amount of heat. Make sure that you have thick clothing that protects the body where the rope will be running, especially where the rope can rub against your neck.

BELAYING

44. HOW TO BELAY

- First of all, find an anchor. This could be a spike of rock, a tree or a jammed stone.
- Make a loop in the main rope and place it over or around the anchor point. The securing loop is formed using a figure-of-eight knot. You can also have a back-up anchor point for extra security.
- Pass the rope over your head (so that it sits above the ropes linked to the anchors) and down to just above the hips, but below the softer part of the waist. Make a twist round the arm closest to the anchor, known as the dead arm. You should have covered arms as well as gloves, to reduce the danger of friction burns.
- Take a seated position, with feet firmly anchored. Make sure the rope between you and the anchor is taut. You and the anchor should be in line with the direction of force. To stop a fall, bring the dead hand across the front of the body. Never take the dead hand off the rope when the rope is being paid out or drawn in. The live hand, nearest the climber, should do this work.

45. HOW TO DIG A SNOW-HOLE SURVIVAL SHELTER

Remember, a snow-hole is a last resort decision. It can take up to two hours to dig depending on the size of the party and drain much needed energy.

It is almost always wiser to use your time and energy to descend from a mountain than to dig a snow hole. However, one of your party may be injured, or there may be other pressing reasons why you cannot do this. If so, the most sensible action is to look for a suitable snowdrift in the lee of a boulder or other natural feature and then make yourself a snow-hole shelter.

SNOW-HOLE

- Cut directly into the drift and then excavate cavities at either side to create the main chamber. Cutting the cavity out in blocks may be quicker than scraping out snow with a small axe.

- Use a rucksack to seal the entrance, which should be slightly lower than the main chamber.

- Make sure that the main chamber is cut in an arch shape so that melt water runs down the sides and does not drip onto sleeping bags and clothing. If you cook inside the shelter, remember that the heat will cause the inside surface of the shelter to melt.

- Remember to have a ventilation hole in the chamber, as well as ventilation through the entrance. Make sure that you keep the ventilation hole clear at all times! Do this by leaving a ski-pole or ice axe in the ventilation hole, which can then be jiggled occasionally to keep the hole open.

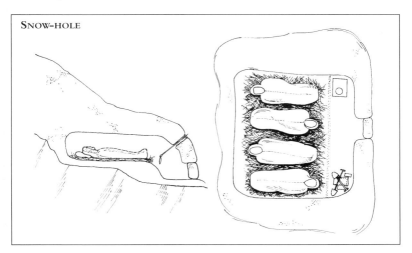

SNOW-HOLE

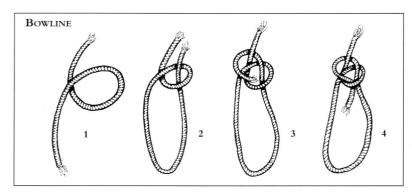

BOWLINE

1   2   3   4

46. MOUNTAINEERING KNOTS

To use mountaineering ropes safely, you need to learn how to tie knots properly. The good news is that for mountaineering purposes you only need to know how to tie two or three different knots. However, it is vitally important that you learn to tie these knots correctly and in all circumstances, including times when you are tired and cold and are more likely to make mistakes. An incorrectly tied knot could lead to an accident. Practice these knots until you can tie them with your eyes closed!

In a survival situation, it will be unlikely that you will have with you all the specialist climbing equipment normally required for safe mountain travel. If you have a rope, then you may need to simply tie people onto the ends of the rope while crossing glaciers or descending steep ground etc. The best knot for this purpose is without doubt the bowline.

To tie a bowline, pass the running end of the rope through the object to be fixed to the bowline and form a loop in the standing part of the rope (1). The running end is then passed through the loop from underneath (2) and around the standing part of the rope (3) and back through the loop from the top (4). The running end passes down through the loop parallel to the rope coming up through the loop. Then pull the knot tight.

Climbers and mountaineers use the Italian hitch to belay fellow climbers, because as a sliding hitch it will absorb the energy and control a fall. The Italian hitch can also be used for lowering an injured person or abseiling. The hitch is reversible by taking the strain off the *loaded* rope and applying it to the *breaking* rope. The former breaking rope becomes the loaded rope, and the former loaded rope becomes the breaking rope.

ITALIAN HITCH

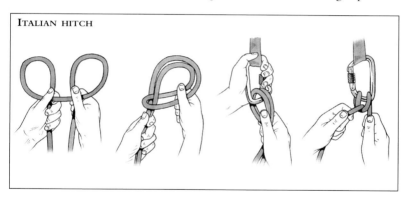

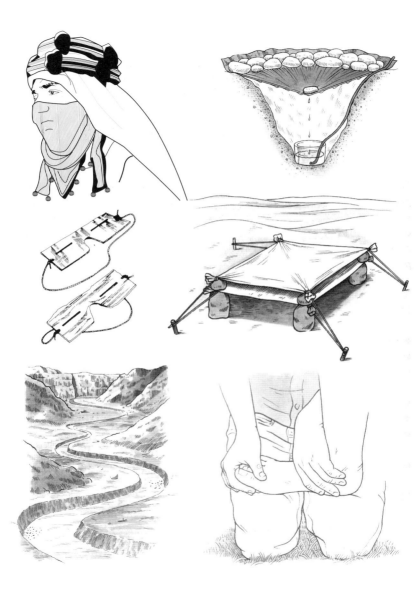

SURVIVING IN THE DESERT

The desert is a place of extremes – extreme heat in the day and freezing temperatures during the night. In addition, there are the perils of blinding glare, sandstorms and, of course, little or no water. Deserts cover about 20 percent of the earth's surface and not all of them are as people think, covered with sand. In fact there are six different types of desert: sand, rock, alkali, rocky plateau and mountain.

There are more than 50 major deserts in the world. Some of the best known are:

- the Arabian – 1,290,000 square km (801,606 square miles)
- the Gobi in Mongolia – 1,040,000 square km (646,256 square miles)
- the Kalahari in southern Africa – 520,000 square km (323,128 square miles)
- the Libyan – 1,680,000 square km (1,043,952 square miles)
- the Mojave in California – 38,850 square km (24,141 square miles)
- the Rub al-Khali, part of the Arabian Desert – 650,000 square km (403,910 square miles)
- the Sahara 37,770,000 square km (23,470, 278 square miles)

CLIMATE
Deserts are characterized by less than 25.4cm (10in) of annual rainfall, an evaporation rate that exceeds precipitation, and a high average temperature.

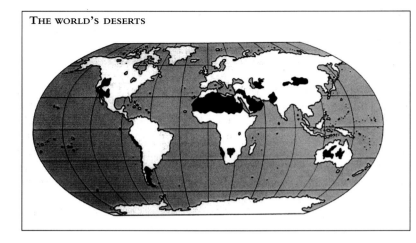

THE WORLD'S DESERTS

No cultivation is possible and perennial plants are confined to watercourses or other places where water accumulates. High pressure causes sparse and irregular rain, clear skies, high temperatures, strong winds and intense evaporation. The little rain that falls is unpredictable – the central part of deserts can receive rain at any time. The lack of moisture in the soil and low humidity in the atmosphere means that most of the sunlight penetrates to the ground. Daytime temperatures can reach 55°C (131°F) in the shade, of which there is little. At night, the desert floor radiates the heat back, causing temperatures to drop to near freezing. The temperature range can be as great as 30°C (50°F), and will vary considerably from one season to another. Frosts may occur during winter months.

LAND AND WATER
Desert terrain varies between mountainous, rocky, sandy, salt marsh and wadi. It is often difficult to traverse on foot, and native peoples do not go

far in the desert without either a camel or some other means of transport. Since the desert soil is unprotected by vegetation, it is easily eroded by wind and water. Water rushing down from hills can form canyons and large slopes of debris. In turn, these slopes level off to form low basins which fill with water when the rain comes.

Flash floods may run off the high ground without warning, and thus be life threatening. This is likely to happen on rocky plateau deserts such as the Golan Heights. Sand dunes can be up to 300m (900ft) high and 24km (15 miles) long. Salt marshes should be avoided. These are flat areas where water has evaporated, leaving an alkaline deposit. Rain erodes sand into canyons and wadis (Arabic for valley or ravine), which can be difficult to traverse. Sandstorms are frequent and, apart from being extremely uncomfortable, they can also cause you to lose your bearings.

Mirages are refractions of light through heated air. The effect they have on objects makes it difficult to assess distances and identify objects.

Travelling in the desert can be extremely hazardous. In daytime, the scorching heat will make movement almost impossible. However, if you are travelling at night in rock or mountainous deserts, you may not see eroded drainage channels and canyons, which could result in you falling and being injured.

47. CLOTHING FOR DESERT TRAVEL

It is a good idea in any environment to follow the example, where possible, of the native people. In North Africa, for example, the Bedouin wear light-coloured, loose-fitting clothing (the hooded cloak is called a burnouse) in order to cover the head and neck for protection against sun, wind and sand. The air trapped between the clothing and the body acts as extra insulation against heat. Even if traditional clothing is not worn, follow the same principles of protection and insulation. You must try to retain sweat on the surface of your body to improve the cooling process. In survival situations, stay clothed and avoid direct sunlight on the skin.

'Army uniform was abominable when camel-riding or when sitting about on the ground; and the Arab things, which I had learned to manage before the war, were cleaner and more decent in the desert.'

(*Seven Pillars of Wisdom,* T.E. Lawrence)

FACE AND EYES

A characteristic of the desert is the blinding glare:

'The particles of sand were clean and polished, and they caught the blaze of sun like little diamonds in a reflection so fierce that after a while I could not endure it. I frowned hard, and pulled the head-cloth forward in a peak over my eyes, and beneath them, too, like a beaver, trying to shut out the heat which rose in glassy waves off the ground, and beat up against my face'.

(*Seven Pillars of Wisdom,* T.E. Lawrence)

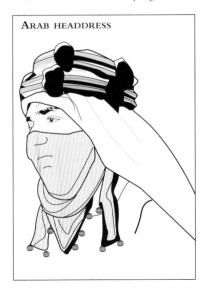

ARAB HEADDRESS

The headdress can be worn to protect the face and eyes by wrapping it round the face, leaving only a small slit for vision. Additional protection can be provided by sunglasses or eye covers, improvised from suitable material, such as cloth or even bark from a tree.

FEET

The desert floor will be either intensely hot or intensely cold, which can cause blistering of the feet and cracking of the heels:

'The sand was still very cold beneath our feet. Usually, when they are in the Sands during the winter or summer, Arabs wear socks knitted from coarse black hair. None of us owned these socks and our heels were already cracking from the cold. Later these cracks became deeper and very painful'.

(*Arabian Sands,* Wilfred Thesiger)

Do not attempt to walk barefoot, as it is unlikely that your feet will be hard enough. If you have shoes or boots, ensure that sand is kept out of them by binding cloth, bandage or other material over the top of the footwear and round the ankle. Check footwear regularly to ensure no sand is inside, as the sand will be abrasive on the feet. Also, check for scorpions and other dangers when putting on footwear.

If the footwear is inadequate (for example, thin-soled), you might be able to improvise by adding an extra layer of protection on the bottom of the shoe (a piece of rubber, perhaps) or inside the shoe (a piece of felt) in order to reduce the heat.

48. HOW TO SHELTER FROM THE SUN

Shelter is your first priority in the desert, both to protect you from the sun during the day and to keep you warm during the intense cold of the night.

The type of shelter you choose will depend largely on your circumstances and the material you have available. If you are near a crashed plane, for example, it is a good idea to build a shelter near the aircraft, as rescuers will be able to spot it relatively easily. Do not shelter inside it, as it is likely to be too hot. If you are near rocky outcrops or caves, these may provide suitable shelter, but beware of unwelcome insects, snakes and other animals that may also be sheltering there.

Before constructing a shelter, first consider the amount of time and energy you have. It is better to build a full shelter in the morning or evening and to improvise temporary shelter during the heat of the day. Do not construct a shelter in a gully in case there are flash floods. Look out for indentations in the ground, which can provide the basis for a shelter.

SANDY AREA SHELTER

To construct this shelter either use the side of an existing dune or build a mound of sand. Anchor your material with weights or plenty of sand on top of the sand bank and extend the material to be anchored at the lower end in the same way.

ROCK OUTCROP WITH CANVAS OR OTHER MATERIAL

Stretch your canvas, poncho or other material from the top of the rocky outcrop to the ground, weighing down each end with stones and sand. Site it in such a way as to minimize the risk of rainwater flowing down the rock and into the shelter.

For either kind of shelter, two layers of material are better than one. Allow a gap of about 40cm (16in) between them and place some light-coloured material on the outside to reflect the sun's rays.

UNDERGROUND SHELTER

This shelter will take more time and should therefore be constructed when the temperature is lower. Find a depression in the ground or a suitable area between rocks, or dig a trench up to 60cm (2ft) deep. Make sure that you will be able to lie in the sunken area comfortably and store any equipment you may have. Place your material over the area. If you have dug a trench, pile the sand round three sides of it to anchor the material, allowing for adequate entry. If you have enough material, place a second layer over the first, with a gap of about 45cm (18in).

SHELTER OPEN ON FOUR SIDES

Similar in principle to the underground shelter, this one is constructed in such a way that all sides are open – in other words, anchored at the four corners of the material.

49. HOW TO FIND WATER

It is vital that a desert survivor finds water. Without it, you will die very quickly indeed. Without water, you can expect to last for only around two-and-a-half days at a desert temperature of 48°C (118°F), and

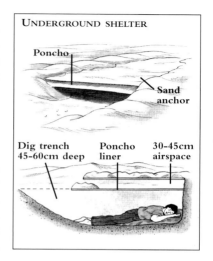

UNDERGROUND SHELTER

Poncho

Sand anchor

Dig trench 45–60cm deep

Poncho liner

30–45cm airspace

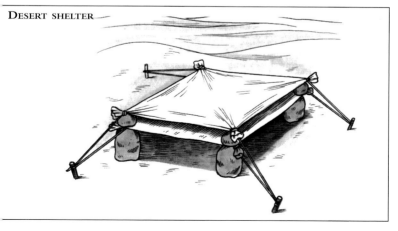

DESERT SHELTER

that is if you have found shade and do nothing but rest! If you decide to walk in a temperature of 48°C (118°F) without water, you will be able to walk about 8km (5 miles) before collapsing. In comparison, in temperatures under 21°C (70°F), you can expect to last up to 12 days.

In the desert, water definitely comes before food. If you have food but little or no water, eat sparingly until a fresh supply of water has been located, as the food you eat will increase the rate at which your body absorbs water. If water is available, work out a sensible ration. Then drink enough at least to clear the head, which will make planning easier.

WATER INDICATORS

Be observant and study the local terrain closely. Seek out the most likely places to find water. Remember that water always flows downhill and generally makes grooves in the earth in the form of creek beds, canyons and washes. It also encourages green vegetation. Look for:

- Areas of vegetation, especially reeds, grass, willows, cottonwoods and best of all, palm trees, which usually indicate permanent water.
- Valleys, gulleys and water courses. Water will normally collect at the lowest point, and on the outside of a bend. Observe the movement of animals, birds and insects. Follow footprints and animal droppings.
- Man-made constructions that might mark a well. Look for mounds (formed of hardened animal excrement) that might mark a water hole
- Clouds, rain and lightning in the distance – head in that direction.
- Walk along the foot of cliffs or outcrops. Water may have collected in depressions or holes in the rocks, in caves and fissures. Look for any signs of moisture or trickling water that may indicate larger supplies. Use a tube to probe into these areas and suck the water out.
- Water sources are sometimes covered by drifted sand in rocky areas. Dig in the areas where water is likely to have collected. If you find brackish (slightly salty) water which looks unpalatable, find the spring

where the water will be fresher. Beware of drinking from desert lakes, they are often salty.

- Remember that in the desert, water may be underground. Find a dry lake or riverbed at its lowest point and dig with a spade, stick or your bare hands if need be. If you start finding wet sand, stop digging and allow the water to seep in.

A Bushman of the Kalahari adopts the following method of finding water. He finds the deepest part of an old watercourse, then digs a hole in the sand to arm's length to find moist sand. He takes a tube almost 1.5m (5ft) long, made from the stem of a bush with a soft core, and winds 10cm (4in) of dry grass lightly round one end. The Bushman then inserts the tube into the hole and packs the sand round it, stamping down the sand with his feet. He sucks on the tube hard for about two minutes, and eventually water comes into his mouth. It should be said that this skill may require a considerable amount of practice to master effectively.

Water can also be extracted from sand or mud by putting it in a cloth and wringing it out into a container. During the rainy season, ensure that any rain is caught. This can be done by staking out or suspending a piece of tarpaulin so that water flows to the centre.

50. HOW TO PREVENT DEHYDRATION

Even in a temperate climate, a minimum of 1.5 litres (2¾ pints) of water is lost by an adult every 24 hours through sweating, breathing and in urine. In a hot climate, as much as an extra 2–5 litres (3½–8¾ pints) of water may be lost, and up to 10 litres (17½ pints) if hard physical exertion is involved. When walking in a temperature of over 38°C (100°F), the sweat loss is 1 litre (1¾ pints) per hour. To reduce water loss:

● Keep perspiration down to a minimum, do not rush around.
● Stay fully clothed; your body will perspire less. You must save every drop of water you have, it is your most valuable possession. If you have had the chance to build a shelter, stay inside it during the hottest part of the day, as this will greatly reduce the rate of water loss.
● Resist the temptation to take large gulps of water – drink water in small sips, not gulps. If water is critically low, use it only to moisten your lips. Keep small pebbles in your mouth or chew grass to relieve thirst.
● Use salt only with water and only if you have a regular water supply.
● Remember, food is less of a priority than water, and it is also equally scarce. Do not eat food unless you have water! Even when you have water, avoid eating proteins that require lots of water for digestion. Remember, too, that foods rich in fat require more water to break them down than foods rich in carbohydrate or starch and sugar.

51. HOW TO MAKE A SOLAR STILL

A solar still is a very good way of producing water. You will require a clear plastic sheet about 2 metres square (6½sq ft), a container to collect the water in a length of plastic tube and some rocks.

First dig out a round hole approximately 1m (3ft) deep and 1 metre (3ft) across. Dig a further small hole in the bottom and place the water con-

WATER INTAKE

Water intake is required every 24 hours to maintain water balance during resting conditions:

°F	°C	US PINTS	UK PINTS	LITRES REQUIRED
95°	35°	8½	7	4
90°	32°	6½	5¼	3
80°	27°	2	1¾	1

As a rule of thumb, if you have 2 US pints/1¾UK pints (1 litre) of water, at a maximum temperature of 110°F (43°C) in the shade, you should last for three and a half days, resting in the shade at all times. If you rest during the day and walk at night (travelling about 25 miles/40km), you should last two and a half days.

tainer in this hole – the wider the container, the more water it will catch. Place one end of the plastic tube in the container and pass the other end over the lip of the hole. Place the plastic sheet over the hole, covering the edges with soil and rocks to anchor it. The sheet should droop into the hole by about 40cm (16in), but should rest clear of the container.

Place a fist-sized stone at the centre of the sheet, directly above the container. Make sure the sheeting does not touch the sides of the hole, otherwise the earth will absorb the condensed water. Within 24 hours, there should be at least 500ml (18fl oz) of water and perhaps up to 1 litre (1¾ pints) in the container. The distillation process makes the water safe to drink. Drink it through a straw.

One still will not keep you alive for a prolonged period of time. If this will be your main source of water, you should construct three or four stills. The upper surface of the still will also catch rainwater, as a bonus.

52. DESERT PLANTS THAT PROVIDE WATER

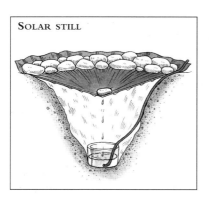

SOLAR STILL

CACTUS

You can cut off the top of a barrel cactus and extract water from the pulp by squeezing or mashing it. Do not eat the pulp, just suck out the juice.

DATE PALMS

Cut at a lower branch near the base. Liquid should ooze from the cut.

BAOBAB TREE

Its large trunk collects water during the rainy season.

PRICKLY PEARS

Their fruit and earlike lobes both contain water.

SAXAUL

This large shrub or tree has a spongy bark containing water. If you press substantial amounts of the bark, you can tap an important source of water in the desert.

ROOTS

The bloodwood desert oak and water tree of Australia have roots lying near the surface which can be cut and sucked to provide moisture.

WATER PURIFICATION

Use purification tablets if you have them (in your survival tin). Boil the water for 10 minutes if you are uncertain of your height above sea level. Add two or three drops of iodine to every 1 litre (1¾ pints) of water and leave to stand for a further 30 minutes.

53. EDIBLE PLANTS

Desert regions produce little in the way of plant food, but what is available provides good eating.

ABAL

Found in North Africa, the Middle East and desert regions of western India, abal has a broomlike appearance, with green branches producing flowers in spring. The flowers are edible.

ACACIA

Mostly native to tropical Africa or Australia, acacia is a spreading, short tree with small leaflets. It has bright yellow balls as flowers and a whitish-grey bark. The young leaves, flowers and pods can be eaten either raw or cooked.

AGAVE

Found in Central America, the Caribbean and parts of the United States and Mexico, this plant has clusters of thick leaves from which a long flower stalk rises. The flowers and flower-buds can be eaten when cooked.

BAOBAB

Found in savannas in Africa, parts of Australia and in Madagascar, its bottle-like trunk can be 9m (27ft) in diameter. The leaves can be made into soup. The fruit, called monkey bread, can be eaten.

DATE PALM

Native to North Africa, southwest Asia and India, the trunk is straight and

AGAVE

rough, and grows to a height of up to 18m (60ft). The leaves are dark green and the fruit, when ripe, is yellow-orange and contains about 58 per cent sugar and 2 per cent each of fat, protein and minerals. The leaves can be used for thatching, and the fibre in the leaf stalks can also be useful (for example, as cordage).

DESERT AMARANTH
The plant appears in many parts of the world. It has alternate leaves and small greenish flowers in clusters at the top of the plant. All parts are edible.

WILD GOURD
This plant appears mainly in the subtropical and tropical parts of the world. The leaves are vinelike, and the young ones can be eaten when cooked. The fruit is about the size of an orange. Seeds should be roasted. The flower can be eaten raw. The stems and shoots can be chewed for water.

CAROB
Found in the Mediterranean, Middle East and parts of North Africa, this tree has compound alternate leaves. The seedpods contain round, hard seeds and a sweet pulp. Young, tender pods can be eaten either raw or boiled. Grind the seeds to make them into porridge.

PRICKLY PEAR
Found in tropical and subtropical areas, these plants have flat-jointed stems covered with small clusters of stiff hairs. The yellow flowers develop into pear-shaped edible fruits.

DESERT GRASSES

All desert grasses are edible. Eat the whitish tender end that shows when it is pulled out of the ground. Grass seeds can also be eaten.

54. DESERT ANIMALS FOR FOOD

The general rule is (with a few exceptions – see Tip 55) that all desert birds, mammals, insects and reptiles are edible. The tricky part is trapping them! Rabbits can be smoked out of their burrows and clubbed as they come out. Look under flat stones for lizards at sunrise. To most people, the thought of eating insects is horrendous. However, in a desert survival situation, eating all the insects you can find will keep you alive. Steer clear of centipedes, scorpions and caterpillars, as some are poisonous.

INSECTS

Insects are a valuable source of protein and can be found in moist, shady spots – for example, under rocks or in caves. Take care, since scorpions, snakes and spiders will also shelter in these areas. Collect crawling insects from under stones. Use a light to attract insects at night.

Remove wings and barbed legs from large insects and take the shell off beetles. They should be cooked before eating to get rid of any parasites. Remove wings and legs and cook grasshoppers before you eat them. Insect larvae are edible; ant larvae make good eating. Insects can be ground into a paste and mixed with vegetation.

REPTILES

These are another good source of protein, but beware of the poisonous varieties, which may lurk in shaded areas, caves and caverns. Edible snakes may be found outside in the cooler parts of the day, but only the non-poisonous varieties should be approached, armed with a forked stick and club. Lizards may fall into a solar still.

MAMMALS

When looking for animals, keep an eye out for obvious signs such as droppings, tracks, trails and feeding areas. Like the reptiles, most desert mammals are largely nocturnal. Rodents should be snared with a loop snare when they emerge at dusk or dawn. Animals like the Arabian Oryx will require a great deal of skill with a spear, or a good shot with a rifle to bring it down. In the Gobi Desert, herds of antelope can be found. Partridge, quail and bustard frequent water sources in the deserts of Iran and Iraq.

Remember, mammals can carry rabies. (For more details, see Tip 147).If you are unfortunate and are bitten, immediately scrub the bite area with soap and water and apply disinfectant (if you have it). If a member of the party has rabies and is in the advanced stage, isolate him or her and tie them down. The person will unfortunately die – do not touch the body after death.

Animals in the advanced stage of rabies, especially dogs, will be violent and will stagger and foam at the mouth. If you are the victim of an unprovoked attack, you should have good reason to suspect that the animal has rabies. Hospital treatment for rabies must start within one or two days to be effective and is very expensive.

55. DESERT ANIMALS TO AVOID!

INSECTS

- Avoid nests of ants (they can be identified as protruding mounds of earth). If you are bitten, a mud pack will sooth the rash and the pain.
- Centipedes should also be avoided: their bites can be painful and the effects can last up to two weeks. They hide under rocks during the day and move about at night.
- Scorpions stay under rocks during the day and move around at night, often into sleeping bags or boots. If you are camping, use a tent with a

sewn-in floor. Shake out your boots in the morning. There is no real field treatment for scorpion stings (the treatment for snake bites is effective – there is an immediate and overall reaction with scorpion stings). Fortunately, most adult victims of scorpion stings recover, though child fatalities are common.

POISONOUS SNAKES

The following poisonous snakes are found in the Americas:

Mojave rattlesnake

Deadly poisonous. Found in: Mojave Desert, California; Nevada; Arizona; Texas; and Mexico. Pale or sandy in colour. Diamond-shaped marks bordered by light-coloured scales and bands around the tail. Length: average 75cm (30in); maximum 1.2m (4ft).

Western diamondback rattlesnake

Dangerously poisonous. Found in: Arizona; south-east California; New Mexico; Oklahoma; and Texas. Light, buff colour with darker brown diamond-shaped markings. The tail has thick black and white bands. Length: average 1.5m (5ft); maximum 2m (6½ft).

The following poisonous snakes are found in Africa and Asia:

Boomslang

Deadly poisonous. Found in sub-Saharan Africa. Green or brown in colour. Boomslangs live in trees and bushes and feed on small animals and birds' eggs. The boomslang has a potent venom that it delivers through large grooved fangs located at the back of its mouth. The bite of the boomslang can be fatal. Length: average 60cm (2ft); maximum 1.5m (5ft).

Egyptian cobra or Asp

Deadly poisonous. Found in: Africa; Iraq; Syria; and Saudi Arabia. Black, yellow or dark brown with brown cross bands. The head is sometimes black. Length: average 1.5m (5ft); maximum 2.5m (8ft).

Horned desert viper
Dangerously poisonous. Found in: Africa; Arabian Peninsula; Iran and Iraq. Pale buff in colour, with a scale over each eye. Length: average 45cm (18in); maximum 75cm (30in).

McMahon's viper
Dangerously poisonous. Found in West Pakistan and Afghanistan. Sandy buff in colour with dark brown spots on body. Broad nose. Length: average 45cm (18in); maximum 1m (3ft).

Palestinian viper
Dangerously poisonous. Found in: Israel; Lebanon; Jordan and Syria.

Puff adder
Dangerously poisonous. Found in: Africa; Israel; Jordan; Iraq and Saudi Arabia. Yellowy, light brown or orange, with chevron-shaped, dark brown or black bars. Length: average 1.2m (4ft); maximum 1.8m (6ft).

Sand viper
Dangerously poisonous. Found in: central Africa; Algeria; Chad; Egypt; Nigeria; Northern Sahara; and Sudan. Pale with three rows of dark brown spots. Length: average 45cm (18in); maximum 60cm (2ft).

Saw-scaled viper
Dangerously poisonous. Found in: Africa; Algeria; Asia; India; Iran; Israel; Jordan; Egypt; Pakistan and Saudi Arabia. Light buff in colour with shades of brown, red or grey. The sides are a lighter colour. Usually two dark stripes on the head. Length: average 45cm (18in); maximum 60cm (2ft).

The following are found in Australasia:

Death adder

Deadly poisonous. In fact the appropriately named death adder is one of the most dangerous snakes in the world. Found in: Australia; New Guinea; and Moluccas. Colour varies between red, yellow and brown, with dark brown crossbands. Tail black at the end. Length: average 45cm (18in); maximum 90cm (3ft).

Taipan

Deadly poisonous. Found in Northern Australia and southern New Guinea. Olive or dark brown in colour, with darker brown head. Length: average 1.8m (6ft); maximum 3.7m (11ft).

Tiger snake

Dangerously poisonous. Found in: Australia; Bass Strait Islands; Tasmania; and New Guinea. Olive or dark brown in colour, with yellow or olive belly and cross bands. The species in Tasmania is black. Length: average 1.2m (4ft); maximum 1.8m (6ft).

POISONOUS LIZARDS
Gila monster

Poisonous. Found in: Arizona; south-east California; New Mexico; Nevada and Utah. It has a large head and heavy tail. Colour: black mixed with yellow and pink. Length: average 30cm (12in); maximum 50cm (20in).

Mexican beaded lizard

Dangerously poisonous. Found in: Mexico and Central America. Has either black or pale yellow bands or is entirely black. Length: average 60cm (2ft); maximum 90cm (3ft).

56. HOW TO COOK IN THE DESERT

Raw meats, vegetation and insects can all be turned into tasty meals – just use a little imagination and any of the following cooking methods:

BOILING

Make a boiling pot by scooping out a hole in hard ground. Line it with leaves or other waterproof material and fill it with water, then drop red hot coals from the fire into it. In mountainous regions, you often find rocks with natural holes and scoops in them made by erosion – these are perfect for use as pots. Preheat the rocks in the fire before filling them with water.

Some large plant leaves can be bent into container shapes then filled with water and held over the fire to boil. The leaves will not burn as long as they are filled with water.

FRYING PANS

Find some flat narrow desert rocks, and lay them across other rocks. Build a fire underneath the flat rocks and when they are hot, wipe any grit off the top surface and start frying your meat or birds eggs.

ROASTING

Skewer your meat on a green stick (dry sticks will burn) and hold near good 'glowing red' embers.

KEBABS

The same as roasting – just cut meat into even cubes and spear them onto a sharpened stick. Roast the kebabs over hot coals.

MUD BAKING

This is a very good way of cooking small animals. Make sure that the animal is gutted and cleaned, but leave the skin or feathers on. Cover the animal in mud or clay at least 3cm (1¼ in) thick. Place in a large fire and cover with coals. It could take up to an hour to cook depending on the size of the animal.

When the clay is baked as hard as a brick, remove it from the fire and break it open. If the animal is cooked, the feathers or skin will beak away at the same time, leaving you with a very tasty meal.

BAKING IN ASHES

Simply rake a hollow in the fire embers, place the animal in the hollow and cover it with the rest of the ashes. Leave to cook.

GRILLING

Dig a hole that is larger and wider than the animal to be cooked and about 1m (3ft) deep. Build a fire in the bottom and wait until it is hot. Place some small stones in the fire to heat up and radiate the heat. Make a grid of green poles over the top and place the meat on top of this to cook.

57. DESERT ILLNESSES

HEAT CRAMPS

Caused by excessive loss of salt through sweating, cramps normally occur in muscles that are being used – for example, abdomen, arms and legs. The symptoms are shallow breathing, vomiting and dizziness. Move the patient into shade and provide water with salt dissolved in it (2 tablets per 1 litre/1¾ pints of water).

HEAT EXHAUSTION

This is characterized by fatigue, dizziness or nausea due to long exposure to heat; the body may have a temperature below normal and there is persistent sweating. The skin is moist and clammy, the pulse weak. First aid involves cooling the person and providing small sips of water. Heat exhaustion can be accompanied by cramps of the extremities, which should be treated by local massage.

HEATSTROKE

Humans will die after losing 12–13 per cent of their weight as body water. When the body dries out, the blood becomes more viscous and cannot circulate around the body adequately. Death from heatstroke occurs when the blood is no longer able to transport the metabolic heat from inside the body to the skin.

Symptoms are: hot, dry skin; no sweat; flushing of the face and feverishness; raised temperature with rapid, strong pulse; severe headache; and vomiting. The victim may become unconscious.

The body temperature must be lowered as soon as possible. Lay the victim in the shade, with the head and shoulders slightly raised. Remove outer clothing, wet the inner clothing and fan the patient. If no water is available, dig a trench in the sand and place the victim in the bottom. When the patient is conscious again, provide water with salt added (2 tablets per 1 litre/1¾ pints of water). First aid must be immediate and the temperature must be brought down to below 39°C (102°F). This can be done by rubbing the victim's skin with cold water or alcohol.

SUNBURN

Sunburn can be dangerous if the victim is overexposed. Make sure the body is adequately protected against the sun. Treat using after-sun cream/rehydrating cream.

SORE EYES

Do not neglect eye protection. Soreness can be caused by a mixture of glare and exposure to flying sand. Treat the eyes with boracic ointment and bandage lightly. If no ointment is available, apply a damp bandage. All desert cuts and sores should be treated with antiseptic ointment as soon as

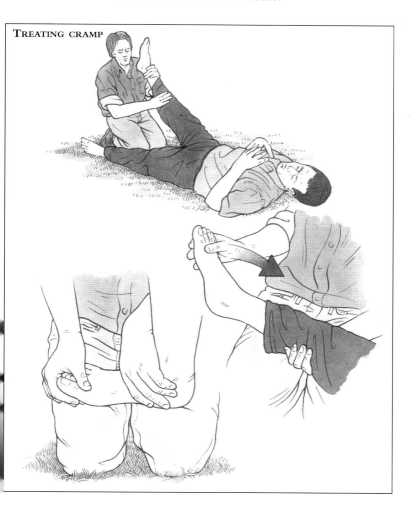

TREATING CRAMP

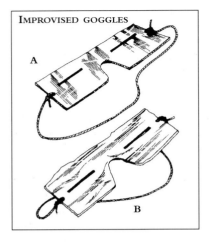

IMPROVISED GOGGLES

possible. Wear sunglasses if you have them; alternatively, improvise a pair of sun shades from cardboard (A) or tree bark (B): make narrow eye slits to reduce glare. Smear soot from the fire below the eyes (rather like American footballers.

In the desert, you are vulnerable to a host of insect-borne diseases, such as malaria, sandfly fever, typhus and plague. You must try to employ preventative medicine measures and adequate personal hygiene and sanitation. Guard against cuts and scratches: in the desert, they can become infected very easily. To prevent intestinal diseases, clean all cooking and eating utensils, dispose of garbage and human wastes and protect food and utensils from flies.

Do not expose your flesh to the elements or to flies; try to wash your feet and body daily, and change your socks regularly. You must check yourself for signs of any injury, no matter how slight. Remember dust and insects can cause infection of minor cuts and scratches.

For sanitary reasons, bury all garbage and human wastes, but remember to bury them deep because shallow holes can become exposed in areas of shifting sands.

58. HOW TO NAVIGATE IN THE DESERT

SETTING COURSE

The desert nights will normally be clear, allowing identification of the Southern Cross, which indicates true south. Once a course has been set, direction should be maintained by compass. Without a compass, desert navigation is problematic, since there are few features to follow. One method is to follow objects that are in direct line with each other, and as far apart as possible. Before one object is reached, a third should be chosen in direct line with the second, and so on.

ASSESSMENT OF DISTANCES

Another difficulty in the desert can be assessing distances. The clear atmosphere makes objects appear closer than they really are. As a rough guide to correction, multiply by three your visual estimation of distance. If possible, use a more accurate method of determining distance.

Mirages can play havoc with navigation. Be especially alert for mirages concealing objects, creating imaginary objects and making red objects seem closer and larger than they really are. Remember that mirages are common during the heat of the day. Interestingly, mirages are also common in the polar regions.

PACING

A proven method of estimating a distance is to measure it through the number of paces taken. The average stride of a man is 75cm (30in), which is 7.5m (23ft), every 10 steps. It is useful to know the length of your own stride, and to practise measuring distances in this way, before embarking on an expedition.

Remember, if your route takes you through sand dunes, it is less taxing to walk on the windward side of the tops of the dunes than walking up and down them in an effort to stay on a straight line course.

TIMING

Another method of estimating distance is by using a watch, working on the knowledge that the average person walks about 4km (3 miles) per hour. Take care to adjust for difficult terrain, such as deep sand.

SURVIVING IN POLAR REGIONS

Polar survival depends on your ability to find adequate clothing and shelter. With these two elements in place, this environment of low temperatures, wind chill, snow and ice can be mastered like any other. Nevertheless, even the best-laid plans can go wrong and the polar climate can kill you very quickly. The polar regions are, by definition, deserts, which means that they each have less than 25.4cm (10in) of annual precipitation. The difference is that at the poles it falls as snow.

Humans have been living happily in polar climates for centuries and have learned how to live alongside nature. By using this vast store of knowledge we can equip ourselves with the skills to master this harsh environment.

The North polar region is a frozen ocean (the Arctic Ocean) surrounded by land. The South polar region (or Antarctic continent) is a landmass lying 3–4km (2–3 miles) above sea level, surrounded by water. This means that it is extremely cold and almost entirely covered by ice, which can be up to 3km (2 miles) thick.

During winter in the polar regions, the sun can remain below the horizon for several months, so that the only source of warmth is wind flowing in from lower latitudes. In the summer, the sun remains low in the sky, providing little heat, although if you are north of the Arctic circle (66°33'N), or south of the Antarctic circle the sun is above the horizon 24 hours a day for part of the summer. At 90° north and south, the region experiences six months of day and six months of night.

The Antarctic continent supports only two species of flowering plant, and the animals in the polar regions are almost entirely dependent on the sea for food. The polar bear lives in the Arctic and birds come in the summer to breed, though they really belong to the tundra regions. There are almost no land animals in the Antarctic, though penguins are found in abundance. Seals can be found in both regions.

59. POLAR CLOTHING

You should take specialist advice on clothing before entering an extreme cold weather or 'deep field' polar environment. There are a wide variety

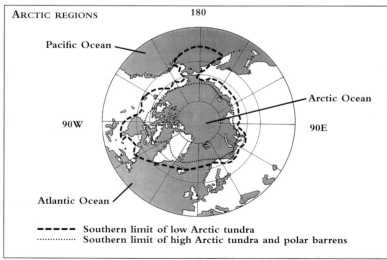

ARCTIC REGIONS

180

Pacific Ocean

Arctic Ocean

90W

90E

Atlantic Ocean

- - - - Southern limit of low Arctic tundra
.... Southern limit of high Arctic tundra and polar barrens

of newly developed fabrics available, including polypropylene under-wear, so there is a reasonable choice.

You need a windproof outer layer, which should also be waterproof to repel melting snow. A breathable fabric such as ventile cotton is ideal. You should also wear inner layers of insulation – several thin layers are better than one or two thick layers. Use a drawstring hood on your jacket and one that is edged with fur, as this will keep wind off your face.

If newly developed fabrics are not available, use wool for the inner lay-ers as it has low water absorbency. Do not wear tight or restrictive cloth-ing, and keep it clean and dry. Loosen or remove items of clothing, such as a hat or gloves, rather than allow yourself to sweat. If you sweat, the cloth-ing will become wet, losing its insulating properties and drawing heat away from the body.

In extreme cold conditions, mitts are much warmer than gloves. If you possess only one pair, make sure that they are connected to you with line or tape as you cannot afford to risk them being blown away or lost.

Waterproof canvas boots known as Mukluks are the ideal polar footwear. Mukluks have a thick (1–2cm/½–¾in) insole that insulates the foot, by stopping cold striking up into the sole of the foot. Ideally you should wear three layers of socks inside your boots, sized in such a way that they fit over each other.

Ski goggles or snow glasses with protective leather side glare protection are essential to avoid snow blindness. If you have only a pair of ordinary sun-glasses, these will provide some protection and you can easily impro-vise side glare protection by using card or any suitable material. If you lose your eye protection, make some improvised goggles immediately! (see illustration of improvised goggles, Tip 57).

If socks and gloves get wet, you can help to dry them out by wrapping them round your stomach. Try to carry as many spare pairs of socks as pos-sible. Dry them over a fire in a shelter if possible, or wrap them around your waist under your clothing.

COLD-WEATHER CLOTHING

Fluff out any down-filled clothing or bedding that has become compressed; it is the air spaces that are all-important in insulation.

Brush off any snow from clothing before entering a shelter or other warm place. Don't get into a sleeping bag with wet clothing. Wear the minimum possible for sleeping and leave clothes out to air and dry. Fluff out and dry the sleeping bag after use, before rolling it up to protect it.

60. SHELTERING FROM THE WIND

First of all, get out of the wind. You cannot expect to stay in the open in winter and survive, unless you are moving. Find shelter that is large enough to provide room for yourself, companions and equipment, but not so large that it will absorb heat from your bodies. The shelter should be compact and snug.

SITE OF SHELTER

Look around you for indicators of prevailing wind direction, such as tail drifts of snow, which form in the lee of rocks, slopes and off mountain ridges. Wind scoops form on the windward side of cliffs. If you have a tent, then make sure that it is well dug in and set with its back to the prevailing wind.

In the winter, do not build shelters in the lee of slopes and cliffs where snow may drift heavily and bury your shelter. In the summer, do not camp on low-lying ground, which is likely to be damp, or in areas that might be susceptible to flooding. Choose a place where there will be a cool breeze to keep insects away.

If you are on sea ice, choose the older, thick ice and shelter on the biggest floe. Older, thicker floes stand higher out of the water than young thin ice. Keep away from thin ice.

Do not use an aircraft or vehicle as a shelter unless it is well insulated, as the metal conducts heat away. A shelter needs to be well ventilated, to avoid the risk of carbon monoxide poisoning, especially if a fire is to be constructed inside it.

61. FINDING NATURAL SHELTERS

Caves and overhanging rock shelves may provide dry shelters. They need to be well insulated in winter, and kept free of insects in summer.

TREE WELL SHELTER

Spruce trees can provide natural shelters in thick snow. Dig a hole round the base of the tree so that the lower branches form a canopy.

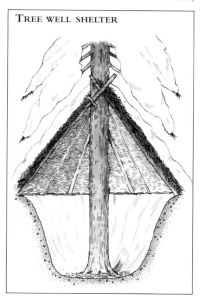

TREE WELL SHELTER

Depending on how long you intend to stay, or how effective the lower branches are as cover, you can erect your own roof with cut branches and boughs, taking care not to disturb the snow on the tree you will be under. Insulate the hole with branches.

LEAN-TO SHELTER

You can sling a horizontal bar between two trees or uprights and lean branches or boughs down the back for shelter, allowing enough space for you to lie inside with equipment. You can cover the roof with sod blocks, which should be arranged like tiles to allow water to run off. You can build snow up on the sides where appropriate to provide extra insulation. Build a fire just outside the shelter, with a reflector made of logs or other material to send the heat into the shelter.

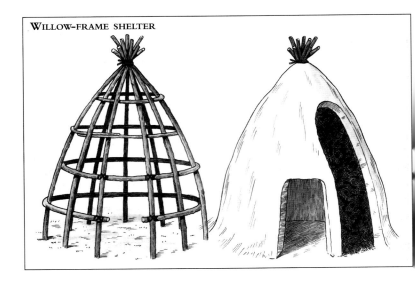

WILLOW-FRAME SHELTER

WILLOW-FRAME SHELTER

This involves constructing a frame from willows, which can be either upright or elongated. The framework can then be covered with parachute material or with branches, overlaid with sods and snow.

FALLEN-TREE SHELTER

Dig out what little snow there is under the tree. If necessary, cut branches from underneath the tree to line the floor.

62. BUILDING SHELTERS FROM SNOW

The ideal snow to make a shelter is firm enough to take a man's weight without a deeply embedded footprint. Blocks when cut should be about 45cm (18in) wide, by 50cm (20in) long, and 8–10cm (3–4in) thick. This will provide insulation and allow light into the shelter.

SNOW TRENCH

This allows you to get below the surface, away from wind and snow. You can use snow blocks for overhead cover as well as for a door.

Mark out a rectangle in the snow. Cut out snow blocks just over 1m (3ft) deep from the marked-out area. Cut an L-shaped step 15cm (6in) deep and 15cm (6in) wide along the top edges and sides of the trench. Lean two blocks together at the opposite end from the entrance to start forming the roof. Make sure they are offset – that is, one of the snow blocks' edges extends beyond the other, so that the next block can be laid in place and supported. Cover each end with a block and dig a burrow-like hole at one end for an entrance. Alternatively, lay the side blocks upright with roof blocks placed horizontally across.

IGLOO OR SNOW HOUSE

Building a good igloo requires a lot of skill and practice, and you will also

SNOW SAW

need something like a snow saw or adequate knife to do the job. Igloos take a lot of time and energy to build, so should be considered only when you are certain that you will need to stay put for several days. Draw a circle of about 2.5–3m (8–10ft) diameter in the snow to mark the inside of the igloo. Cut snow blocks from a nearby trench. When you have about 12 blocks, you can start building.

Place blocks in a circular row with the side faces of each block angled to the centre of the igloo, and the tops of the blocks sloping inwards. Shave the tops of this row of blocks in a sloping angle to form the first rung of a spiral. Start the next row of blocks, cutting the blocks in such a way as to make the igloo curve inwards. When placing the key block, the hole should be longer than it is wide so that the block can be passed up through the hole and allowed to settle back into position. Pour powdery snow over the structure to seal any gaps. The Inuit sometimes insert a clear sheet of ice as a window.

Inside the igloo, cut a subterranean entrance, a sleeping level and a cooking level. You will need insulation on the sleeping level. Place sleeping bags so that the head is nearest the entrance. Use a snow block for the door, which should be left open during the day. Remember to insert ventilation holes.

MOULDED DOME SHELTER

This shelter requires less expertise and time to construct than, for example, an igloo. Fill a poncho or other large piece of material with bark and small boughs. Cover the material with snow, leaving a gap for the entrance.

BUILDING AN IGLOO

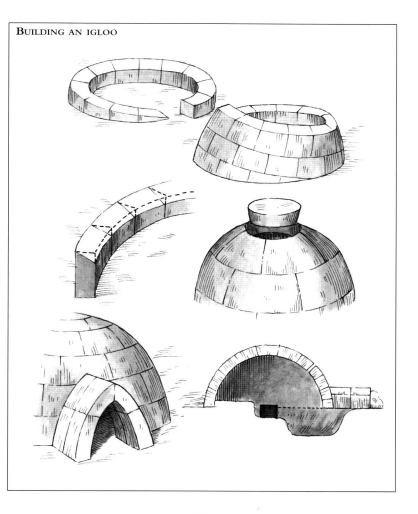

When the snow has hardened, remove the material and contents, thus creating a living space. Insulate the floor with green boughs and make an entrance block with a smaller amount of material filled with small sticks and rubble.

63. HOW TO LAY OUT A CAMP

Choosing your campsite with care can reduce the risk of bear visits. Avoid the following areas:

- Close to an active glacier front
- Heavily pressured ridges of sea ice
- Along the shore lines
- Near to known polar bear den sites
- Locations where there are signs of bears (for example, tracks or fresh droppings).
- Locations where loud noise (from outwash rivers, for example) would drown the sound of an approaching bear.

CAMP LAYOUT

Give special thought to the arrangement of tents and shelters to make your camp safer should a bear come to investigate. Remember that:

- A few big tents or shelters are better than several small ones, and sleeping quarters should preferably be around 50m (150ft) upwind from the cooking and waste disposal areas – check prevailing wind direction.
- Garbage should be burned well away from the camp (at least 200m/600ft), but in an area visible from the camp.
- Latrines should be located at least 50m (150ft) downwind from the sleeping quarters.

64. HOW TO PRODUCE HEAT FOR WARMTH AND COOKING

Use any fire-making equipment in your emergency pack, or a stove you may be carrying. To make a fire, you will need to construct the right kind of base and also find kindling and fuel.

Do not build the fire under a snow-covered tree or near anything that is likely to put it out. The fire should be constructed on a firm platform, which you can make out of stones or green wood logs. Failing that, you can dig down to firm soil. If you want to cook, construct a frame to concentrate the heat and to hang a pot on. If you want to heat a shelter, construct a reflector.

FUEL

Pick up kindling during the day wherever you can find it. Dead trees are best for fuel, though birch will burn if split, and green wood will burn on a hot fire. Cassiope is a plant used by the Inuit for fuel when there is no other wood. Other fuels to use are peat, animal dung and even dry grass twisted together.

In 'deep field' polar situations, natural fuel such as wood is non-existent. You will need some other form of fuel, such as gasoline, kerosene or diesel oil, and a stove to burn it. Without it, your life expectancy will be very short. Your only chance is to hunt and kill a seal. Seals provide blubber that will burn as well as food. Immediately after killing the seal, break open the skull and eat the brains while they are still warm. This will extend your survival time long enough for you to collect sufficient fuel (blubber) and meat to survive for several days.

LIGHTING THE FIRE

Make sure everything is easily to hand before attempting to light the fire. If you have matches, use one to light a candle or a bundle of sticks with which you can then light the fire. When kindling is lit, gradually add the fuel, without packing it too densely. Blow on the fire if necessary.

Remember that when your hands are very cold and numbed, they are less sensitive to heat. This could result in you burning your hands without even knowing it.

65. HOW TO AVOID CARBON MONOXIDE POISONING

This is particularly dangerous in extreme cold climates because shelters are likely to be small and well sealed against the elements, increasing the risk of insufficient ventilation. Good ventilation is absolutely essential if you are forced to light a stove or build a fire inside your tent or shelter. Carbon monoxide, which is both colourless and odourless, will be given off by any gas or stove.

SYMPTOMS

These are difficult to detect, especially when they are happening to you, but will include slight headache, dizziness, drowsiness, nausea and, possibly, vomiting; the patient may also suddenly fall unconscious.

TREATMENT

Remove the patient to fresh air or a well-ventilated area and get him/her to breathe deeply. If the person is unconscious, apply artificial respiration in a well-ventilated area, and give oxygen if available. When recovered, the patient should be allowed to rest and be given warm drinks. The patient should not undertake heavy work until fully recovered.

PREVENTION

Keep all shelters well ventilated, which means having at least two ventilation holes to allow circulation. Do not let fires burn up too high. Make sure all stoves burn with a clean blue flame. Turn off all stoves and lamps before going to sleep, otherwise you may not wake up!

66. FINDING WATER

There is no lack of water in polar regions, but the quantity of water obtained from snow and ice will depend on the amount of fuel available to melt it. It is preferable to melt ice rather than snow, as the volume of water will be greater. Do not sacrifice water intake to save fuel – this will lead to dehydration and eventually to serious side-effects. Instead, limit the amount of water lost through sweat by loosening or removing clothing when working.

In the summer, water can be obtained from streams, lakes and ponds. Large snow patches on hillsides will produce small rivulets of water that can be collected. In tundra regions, the water may be stained brown by vegetation, but it is still fit to drink. Despite the fact that water in polar regions is, comparatively, cleaner than in other regions of the world, you should still purify water before you drink it and, if necessary, strain it. You will also find that arctic streams become infested with mosquito larvae in late summer. These larvae are harmless, but it is still better to boil or strain the water before drinking.

WATER MACHINE

In winter, you can obtain water most easily from lakes under the ice and snow. Since the lower surface of the ice follows the contours of the surface of the snow above it, you should dig where the snow is deepest and then chip through the ice under this to find the least cold water.

When heating snow, melt a little at a time and wait until it is fully melted before adding more. Otherwise, the unmelted snow will draw up the water and the pot will burn.

Old sea ice yields much better drinking water than young ice, which will still be salty. Old sea ice will be rounded and have a bluish tinge.

Do not fill your water bottle right to the top with water – you need to allow some movement in the water to prevent it freezing again. Keep the water bottle close to your body to prevent freezing.

BLACK BAG METHOD

On bright sunny days, water can be produced by filling a black plastic bag (bin liner or similar) with snow and hanging it up in the sun. The black bag will absorb heat radiation from the sun and melt the snow inside the bag even when the outside temperature is well below freezing.

67. FINDING FOOD

Ideally, you should have at least two hot meals a day in an extremely cold environment, as well as an occasional hot drink. This will enable your body to generate heat. Food is not abundant in polar regions, though in summer months you should easily be able to obtain fish and other water life from coastal waters, streams, rivers and lakes. You should be able to find clams, crawfish, mussels, snails, limpets, chitons, sea urchins and King Crab on most Arctic shores. Look for streams and inlets that lead to inland lakes, as these make good spawning grounds for arctic char during the summer months.

Do not eat dead shellfish. The small black-purple mussel of the northern Pacific waters is poisonous and should be avoided. Do not eat fish that have sunken eyes, slimy gills, flabby flesh or skin, or an unpleasant smell. Do not eat any kind of jellyfish. Kelp and other smaller seaweed are edible, though you should avoid seaweed that has long filaments and tendrils.

ICE FISHING

Sea ice may be as much as 4m (13ft) thick, so you will need to choose an appropriate spot to create a borehole for fishing, where the ice is not too thick to make a hole but thick enough to bear your weight. You can dangle a line on the end of a small stick with some form of signalling device attached to it, such as a handkerchief or piece of card. Tie this stick to another that is across the fishing hole. When a fish bites, it should cause the pennant to spring up.

ICE FISHING

SEALS FOR FOOD

A large seal can provide enough meat to keep you alive for many weeks. In the Antarctic, seals can be approached on the ice and easily shot. This is due to the fact that Antarctic seals have no predators when they are out of the water. In the Arctic, however, it is a different story: seals are hunted by man and have become very difficult to approach.

In spring, earless seals can be found basking on the ice near their breathing holes. They are extremely vigilant, however, and difficult to hunt. You are only likely to be able to kill a seal with a clear shot to the brain, and preferably before it slides into the water, as it will be very difficult to retrieve.

Take care that you are not stalked by a polar bear, which may be able to smell the blood of a newly killed seal.

PLANTS FOR FOOD

The following plants grow in arctic and sub-arctic regions, though bear in mind that almost all plants found in these regions are smaller than those found in more temperate zones. Tundra vegetation has few species that are edible. Some mushrooms are edible.

Look out for where animals and particularly birds are feeding, as this will lead you to vegetation. Also, when walking, pick up any edible vegetation you see so that you gradually accumulate enough for a meal.

ARCTIC WILLOW

Found in tundra regions of North America, Europe and Asia. Forms in mats with rounded leaves and yellow catkins. It is high in vitamin C and you can eat raw the inner portion of the new shoots as well as the young roots. Both need peeling.

BEARBERRY

Found in Arctic and temperate regions. Forms mats with club-shaped leaves and pink or white flowers. The red berries can be eaten raw or cooked and you can make tea from its leaves.

CROWBERRY

Found in tundra regions of North America and Eurasia. A small shrub with needle-like, evergreen leaves. It has small, black berries, which can be eaten raw or dried for later use. The Inuit eat the black crowberry either raw or mixed with animal oil.

FIREWEED

Found in wood and beside streams and seashores in Arctic regions. Tall with pink flowers and fine leaves. The leaves, stems and flowers are edible, but are best in spring before the plant becomes tough.

ICELAND MOSS

Found exclusively in the Arctic in open areas. Can be a variety of grey-green, white or brownish red. All parts are edible but should be soaked, then thoroughly boiled.

MARSH MARIGOLD

Found in the Arctic and sub-arctic regions in bogs, lakes and some streams. Rounded, dark green leaves on a short stem and yellow flowers. All of the plant is edible but should be boiled.

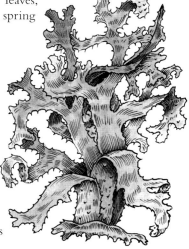

ICELAND MOSS

REINDEER MOSS

Found in open, dry areas. It has hollow, grey stems and antler-like branches. All of the plant is edible but should be soaked for several hours before boiling thoroughly.

ROCK TRIPE

Some of the larger black lichens are edible, and are known as rock tripe. They have been used for food by starving explorers. Rock tripes can be found on stones and boulders. The plant has a rounded appearance with curling edges. The top of the plant is normally black, the underside lighter. All of the plant is edible, though it can be an irritant if eaten raw. You should soak for a lengthy period, change water and boil well; roast as well to make it crunchy.

SPATTERDOCK OR YELLOW WATER LILY

Found in shallow calm water. Has yellow flowers, which develop into bottle-shaped fruits. All of the plant is edible. Seeds can be roasted and ground for flour. The root can be boiled.

ROCK TRIPE

68. AVOIDING POLAR BEARS

Polar bears are normally found near the coast and should be treated with extreme caution. Despite their awesome size and strength, polar bears can be fast and agile over rough ground and are excellent swimmers. Polar bears are curious by nature and will go out of their way to investigate anything out of the ordinary. They have a very acute sense of smell and eyesight, which is thought to be equal to that of a human. Do not underestimate their ability to find carelessly stored food – never keep food in the sleeping tents or shelters or you could find yourself with an unwelcome visitor!

Polar bears are the largest carnivore on land. Seals, and especially ringed seals, make up the major part of the polar bears' diet, but they are often attracted to the things that people bring to the Arctic, such as rope, tents, rubber (boats), engine oil and garbage.

Remember, keep the camp clean and try to produce as little waste as possible. Eliminate or reduce food odours and maintain special areas for cooking and storing food. Seal leftovers in an airtight container and use them up as soon as possible. Grease, oil and fat smell good to polar bears. Store it in airtight containers.

From early March until about mid-October, bears are active and may be seen in coastal and drift ice regions. Between October and March, all polar bears stay in winter hibernation dens in snow banks. Always remember that during the summer months when coastal drift ice is absent, polar bears will visit inland valleys searching for food.

CONSTRUCTING A TRIP-WIRE BEAR ALARM

A basis trip-wire system can easily be set up around your campsite. Use electrical wire, fishing line, rope or string to construct a low (60cm/2ft) fence. The ends of the line can be attached to anything that will make a loud noise, such as a pile of empty tins or fuel cans, electric alarms or blank 12 gauge shotgun cartridge firers. The fence should surround the entire camp and be far enough away from the tents to give you time to respond to the warning.

HOW TO DETER POLAR BEARS

Polar bears are unpredictable and while one bear can be easily chased away, another may be impossible to scare and become a threat to you.

● Make lots of noise by shouting and banging pots and pans.

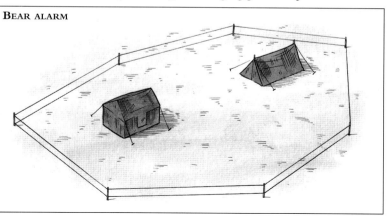

BEAR ALARM

- Fire a pencil flare gun directly at the bear. It makes a loud bang and a hissing noise, and can be quite effective. However, I have heard stories of bears eating the flare while it is still burning!
- Thunderflashes are very portable and easy to handle. When throwing, try to hit the bear or the ground directly in front of it. Remember, the range is dependent on the strength of your arm.
- Warning shots from a rifle have been known to deter bears, but bears live in an environment where loud bangs are an everyday noise: ice floes crack and bank, icebergs break up with loud bangs. I have tried this method and the bear took no notice of the shots, but other bears may respond differently. Avoid hitting the bear. Remember, bullets can ricochet off ice, rocks and frozen ground, and more importantly, remember that each shot fired is one shot less in your rifle!

69. HOW AND WHEN TO SHOOT A POLAR BEAR

When to shoot a bear is a very difficult and very personal decision to make, and must be made very quickly. The right moment to pull the trigger has a great deal to do with your experience and confidence at handling a rifle, how fast the bear is coming at you, and, most importantly, your nerve!

Everyone will react differently when faced with a charging polar bear. It is generally recommended to wait until the bear is 10–15m (30–45ft) away from you before shooting. An accurate shot fired at close range has a much better chance of killing a bear than a shot fired from a distance.

WHERE TO AIM

If you decide to kill the bear, make sure you do it cleanly and with the first shot if possible. Kneel down and aim for:

- The low neck if the bear is broadside to you.

● Low centre neck between the shoulder blades if the bear is facing you.
● If the bear is approaching you half broadside, aim for the front shoulder area to knock the bear down and disable it.

Do not aim at the head, as this kind of shot often does not kill a bear. After your first shot, don't stop to admire your work: if the bear goes down, fire more shots into its vital areas until it is still. Make sure it is dead!

WHAT IF YOU WOUND A BEAR?

A wounded bear is very dangerous indeed. Tracking a wounded bear is not a task that you should have to do. However, should you injure a bear, it becomes your responsibility to find and kill it.

Never track a wounded bear alone – there should be at least two armed people. Be prepared for a close encounter with a very angry bear!

Obviously, in a true survival situation, you may not have the time or the desire to chase off after a wounded bear. Your choice will more than likely be dictated by the circumstances of your situation.

70. HOW TO SURVIVE BY PLAYING DEAD

Playing dead could prevent serious injury if you are involved in a surprise encounter that brings on an attack, and you are unable to kill the bear. Do not play dead if the bear has been stalking you and appears to consider you as its next meal!

Playing dead may reduce your apparent threat to the bear. If you appear as something harmless, the bear may leave. Should the bear attack, playing dead will help protect the vital areas of your body. Curl up into a ball and lie on your side with your legs drawn up to your chest and your head buried in your knees. Grip your hands together behind your neck. Keep your legs tight together and try to stay in this position even if the bear moves you.

Try your best not to resist or struggle, as this may intensify the attack. Make absolutely sure that the bear has gone before moving.

71. ANIMALS OF THE TUNDRA

Tundra is the name for large areas of northern Asia and Canada covered by treeless vegetation.

ARCTIC HARES
These animals forage throughout the winter.

CARIBOU
Live in the far north of Canada and make distant migrations.

LEMMING
The most common small herbivore of the tundra. Lemmings migrate, and many famously meet their end when trying to negotiate water barriers.

MUSKOX
Muskoxen are potentially dangerous animals. Do not approach muskoxen closer than about 25m (85ft). Never corner a muskox; always leave an easy escape route open for the animals if you try to approach them. The months of August and September are the rutting season and you should therefore stay clear of lone bulls that you may see during these months. If you have to pass groups of muskoxen on a hillside, always pass on the downhill side. Muskox can run uphill very fast indeed, but have difficulty running downhill especially on scree slopes.

In areas of the Arctic with high density of muskoxen, you will often be able to see distinct muskox trails in the landscape. These paths are used by the animals to travel between preferred feeding areas. Camping on or close to these trails will only increase the likelihood of encountering problems with muskoxen.

Muskoxen do not migrate, but brave the winter months within the Arctic Circle.

REINDEER
Eurasian equivalent of the caribou; migrates south each winter.

There are a number of predators living in the region:

ARCTIC FOX
Another common predator, which, like the stoat, turns white in winter.
   Arctic foxes are scavengers and often follow polar bears, cleaning up the scraps that they leave. They will also steal any food they can, so make sure all your food is safely stowed away out of their reach.

STOAT
Preys on lemmings and their numbers rise and fall accordingly.

WOLF
Preys on the caribou and follows its path of migration.

Many birds can also be found in the region:

AUKS
These are deep divers that feed on fish.

GOOSE
Common in the Arctic area, where they breed in the summer.

GYR FALCON
Also preys on ptarmigan and grouse.

ARCTIC FOX

GULLS
Sometimes rest inland.

PTARMIGAN
Remains in the Arctic all year round. Hens dig shallow burrows in open ground, in which they lay 8–13 eggs.

SEA DUCK (INCLUDING EIDERS)
Dive to the bottom to find food.

SNOWY OWL
Preys on ptarmigan and grouse.

SWAN
Also breed in summer.

TERNS
The Arctic tern breeds in southern parts of the Arctic and winters in the Antarctic.

WADERS
Shorebirds that search for food in shallow waters.

WILLOW GROUSE
Also remains in the Arctic.

72. ANIMALS OF THE TAIGA

Taiga is the name for swampy coniferous forest that merges into the tundra region in the north and into deciduous forest or grassland in the south. The Taiga extends from northeastern Europe across Russia to the Pacific

Ocean, and across North America from Alaska to Newfoundland. Much of the taiga is north of the Arctic Circle and, although its winters may be just as cold as tundra regions, the summers tend to be warmer. There are a number of animals which are native inhabitants of the taiga, many of which can be killed for food.

MOOSE
The largest deer in the world. Eurasian version is the elk.

SHREWS
Remain active throughout the winter.

SQUIRRELS
Remain active throughout the winter.

TREE PORCUPINE
Found in North America, and also remains for the winter.

VOLES
Red-backed voles live in burrows; climb well.

WOOD LEMMING
Hibernates during the winter.

There are a number of predators living in the region:

LARGE STOAT OR ERMINE
Turns white in winter.

LYNX
Nocturnal predator approximately 80–100cm (32–40in) long.

MARTENS
These weasel-like carnivores are also capable of climbing well.

WEASELS
Medium brown above, white or cream below. Northern species (stoats) moult into white in winter.

Several birds can be found in the region:

EURASIAN CAPERCAILLIE
The capercaillie is the largest of the grouse family.

WOODPECKERS
The northern three-toe woodpecker ranges across the sub-arctic Northern hemisphere.

73. POLAR TRAVEL TECHNIQUES

The decision to travel when in a survival predicament should be based on the likelihood of reaching safety before rescuers find you. Do not move if you are near a large object like a crash-landed plane.

Other factors include the weather and your own physical condition. You should not venture out in a blizzard. If a blizzard is threatening, you need to be fully aware that travel will involve plenty of physical exertion and an increased amount of food and water. You will also need to be able to build temporary shelters en route.

When crossing thin ice, lie flat and crawl so as to distribute your weight. The air in polar regions is very clear, which makes it difficult to estimate distances, as in deserts; underestimating distances is a common problem. Make camp early to allow adequate time to build a shelter. Use snowshoes if the snow is deep. These can be made out of willow.

You will need to be able to determine your present position as well as your intended route.

74. HOW TO NAVIGATE IN POLAR REGIONS

Since the development of the GPS (global positioning system), navigation across featureless polar terrain has become very simple. However, if you are stranded in the Arctic you are unlikely to have a GPS unit handy and will be forced to navigate by other means (Navigation and Signalling, page 235).

STARS

In the northern hemisphere, true north can be gauged from the constellation of Ursa Major (Great Bear), which points to the North Star, standing almost exactly over the North Pole. In the southern hemisphere, the Southern Cross indicates the direction of south. You cannot estimate your latitude from the North Star's height over the horizon to any degree of accuracy without a sextant and a set of tables.

SUN

If you have the correct local time, the shadow cast by a straight object perpendicular to the ground at midday will indicate north and south.

SKY MAP

Observing distant clouds above land and sea can give you plenty of useful information to aid navigation and route planning. Clouds over snowless ground or water will appear black, and produce 'water sky', while clouds over snow or sea ice will be white, producing 'ice-blink'.

BIRDS

Sea birds generally fly out to sea in the morning and return to land in the afternoon.

FLORA

Moss will be thickest on the north side of rocks or trees. Alder bark is lighter on the south side. Lichens are more numerous on the south side.

75. HOW TO AVOID DEHYDRATION

Many survival experts will tell you not to eat snow. This is true to some extent, as eating unmelted snow will lower the body's temperature. However, in a survival situation, take snow into your mouth and allow it to melt and warm before swallowing. This can keep dehydration at bay until you can find other sources of water.

Too many layers of clothing can mean that you will sweat and become dehydrated. Continuously adjust your clothing so that, if anything, you are a little on the cool side rather than too hot.

SYMPTOMS

Urine is a thick yellow colour, and a headache is developing.

TREATMENT

Ensure that you drink enough water to restore the balance. You will know that you are all right, and that the water has filled your cells, when your urine is clearer and your headache has gone. Allowing yourself to become dehydrated will affect your ability to think and plan.

76. HYPOTHERMIA – HOW TO RECOGNIZE AND TREAT IT

This means that the body temperature is below normal. Injury and illness due to cold quite often 'creep up' on you without you realising it.

The body core temperature falls below its normal level of 37.4°C (100°F) when it becomes unable to maintain sufficient heat production.

There are two types of hypothermia: immersion, rapid core cooling due to the conductivity of water; and exposure, slow cooling, either indoors or outdoors.

SYMPTOMS

As the body core temperature falls, the following signs and symptoms will be seen:

- 37°C (100°F) normal body temperature
- 35°C (95°F) shivering, person looks and feels cold.
- 34°C (93°F) changes in personality, 'switching off'
- 33°C (91°F) shivering stops, lowered consciousness level
- 32°C (90°F) limbs stiffen
- 31°C (88°F) rapid decent into unconsciousness
- 30°C (86°F) fixed, dilated pupils
- 29°C (84°F) heart rate become irregular – 'fribulation'
- 24°C (75°F) death

TREATMENT

Return the body to normal temperature as soon as possible. Ideally this should be by immersion of only the torso in warm water at 37.7–43.3°C (100–110°F). Care should be taken with this treatment, as total immersion in warm water could result in shock and cardiac arrest. If warm water is not available, warm the person up in air at around 25°C (77°F).

In a survival environment, the most likely cure is to wrap the patient in a sleeping bag with someone who is warm. Ideally, both should be naked. Do not delay too long. Once the person is conscious, start to give him/her hot, sweetened fluids.

It is not enough simply to remove the patient from the source of heat after the body temperature has returned to normal, as the patient is apt to revert to a low temperature once he/she is removed from the source of heat. Allow the patient to regain a reserve of body heat by keeping him/her warm and administering hot drinks as necessary.

PREVENTION

Do not allow yourself or others to undergo continuous periods of cold without food, hot drinks or other sources of warmth, and beware the danger of getting wet, especially in a wind.

If you fall into water in polar regions, swim violently and rapidly to land. Roll yourself in snow, which will absorb some of the water, and get yourself to a shelter and warmth as fast as possible.

Brush off loose snow before entering the shelter, then dry your clothing and take hot drinks and food.

77. AVOIDING FROSTBITE AND FROSTNIP

SYMPTOMS

This is a serious injury to the skin and sometimes other body tissues by freezing or by formation of ice crystals in the tissue cells. It usually occurs when the temperature is below −12°C (10°F), but can occur at around 0°C (32°F) when there is a wind-chill factor or when the patient has got wet. Since the cold has an anaesthetic effect, frostbite may not be immediately noticed by the victim.

Frostbite normally affects those parts of the body that have the least protection, extremities such as the face, nose, ears, hands and feet. The first signs are a dull white 'waxy' colour in the skin (frostnip), then the formation of blisters, followed by the death of some skin cells and underlying tissue (frostbite).

You should always be watching the faces of your companions for signs of frostnip. If you see any white areas appear on their skin, first tell them and then warm the area with the palm of your hand until the whiteness disappears.

WIND CHILL

Wind chill is a measure of the cooling effect of wind. Wind increases the rate at which the body loses heat, so the air on a windy day feels cooler than the true air temperature.

The effects of wind chill are greater when the air is colder and the wind is blowing harder. With a wind speed of 48km/h (30mph) and an air temperature of −10°C (−23°F), the wind chill equivalent temperature drops to −34°C (−29°F). In very cold weather, exposure to this kind of excessive cooling due to wind chill can lead to frostbite or hypothermia, a lowering of the body temperature that can bring on collapse and death.

TREATMENT

Warm up the affected area and ensure that it does not freeze again. Put affected hands inside clothing near the body; and place affected feet inside a companion's clothing. Do not burst blisters, but dust them with antiseptic powder. Cover the affected area with surgical dressing. Do not dip the affected area into hot water or try to warm by a fire − use body warmth instead. If the casualty is in great pain, consider using morphine.

Serious cases of deep frostbite should be treated by trained medical personnel (see Survival first aid, page 255).

PREVENTION

Try not to wear tight clothing, which reduces circulation and increases the risk of frostbite. Keep out of the wind as far as possible, and always wear adequate dry clothing when going outside.

Move limbs as far as possible, and warm the face by making expressions and exercising the facial muscles. Do not touch cold metal with bare hands, and take special care if you are tired and low in energy.

Do not allow yourself to be splashed with gasoline (petrol) on bare flesh. The evaporation causes 'super-cooling' and almost instant frost damage to the flesh.

78. SKIN-WARMING TECHNIQUES

The efficiency of this is best tested on your hands. If they are particularly cold, first touch them against a warm part of your body to gauge their temperature, then practice the following technique:

- First, imagine that the blood vessels in your hands have become wide open and that hot blood is pumping right through the hands and into the fingertips.
- While you are doing this, also imagine that you are immersing your hands in a thick, very warm orange liquid.
- Finally, while doing the above, actually look at your hands and believe that you have total control over all your bodily processes.

After one or two minutes, the temperature of your hands should be warm, even hot if done well. Oriental practitioners of martial arts such as aikido and chi gong have long demonstrated the power of bodily temperature change, a practice that is just starting to become accepted in the West.

79. TRENCH FOOT – HOW TO TREAT IT

SYMPTOMS
Long exposure to cold and wet can cause feet to turn pale, numb, cold and stiff. The feet will begin to swell, making walking painful. This condition can be serious, so make sure feet and footwear are dried as soon as possible.

TREATMENT
Handle feet with care – do not rub or massage. Clean with soap and water, dry the feet and then keep them raised. Do not walk if you are suffering from this condition. Put on dry socks and make sure there is always a spare, dry pair available.

PREVENTION

Keep footwear as dry as possible and change socks frequently.

80. SNOW BLINDNESS – HOW TO TREAT IT

This is caused by the intense glare of the sun, which is reflected off the snow or intensified by ice crystals in clouds.

SYMPTOMS

Sensitivity to glare. Pinkish vision and watering eyes. Intensifying of reddening vision and pain like grit in the eyes. Loss of vision behind painful, red curtain and sharp pain.

TREATMENT

Urgently place bandage over the eyes and/or place the patient in a dark place. A cool, wet bandage may help relieve the pain. Time is required for the eyes to recover.

PREVENTION

Wear sunglasses. If sunglasses are not available, improvise eyeshades (see Tip 57) by cutting slits in bark or some other material and placing them over the eyes. Rubbing charcoal from the fire or soot from your stove into the skin around the eyes will help to reduce glare.

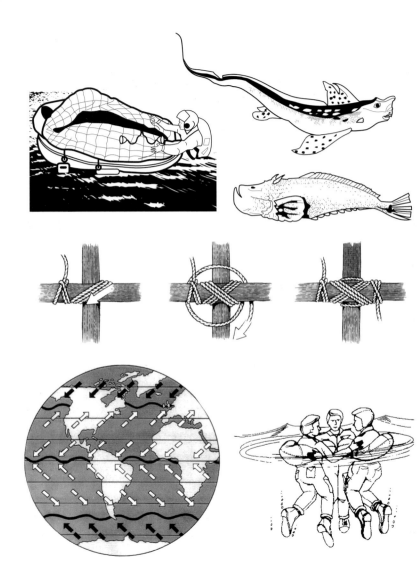

SURVIVING AT SEA

Our natural domain is on land, but this amounts to only around 30 per cent of the earth's surface – seas and oceans cover the other 70 per cent. Therefore, if we are to explore the seas, we must learn how to survive in this dangerous environment that allows little room for error.

OCEAN TEMPERATURE

The temperature of surface water in the ocean can range from 26°C (80°F) in tropical regions to −1.4°C (29°F), the freezing point of seawater, in polar regions. Around 50 per cent of total ocean water has temperatures between 1.3°C (34°F) and 3.8°C (39°F).

81. PREPARATION

- In survival circumstances it is better to retain clothing when in the water. If abandoning a ship or aircraft, take whatever warm clothing is available.

- Wrap a towel around your neck (to prevent heat loss) and take a torch if one is available. Do not jump into the water with an inflated life jacket, as the impact may be dangerous.

- If time allows, fill containers with clean water and stow them on the lifeboat or life raft. A person can last for several days at sea without food, but without clean water to drink, your life expectancy is very limited.

- As you will have no idea how long you will have to survive for before you are rescued or make landfall, try to grab as much canned food as possible before boarding the life raft. Many canned foods, in particular canned vegetables, contain a lot of valuable water. Most life rafts have can openers, but take another just in case! Also take food that is easily portable (for example, chocolate and sweets).

All boats that sail in open water should carry a life raft. A boat larger than fourteen feet should have at least one, but smaller boats may carry only life jackets.

82. HOW TO BOARD A LIFE RAFT

Remember, it is far safer to stay with your boat (even if it is disabled and drifting) than to take to the life rafts. But if you are sinking, you have no choice and should know how to use a life raft.

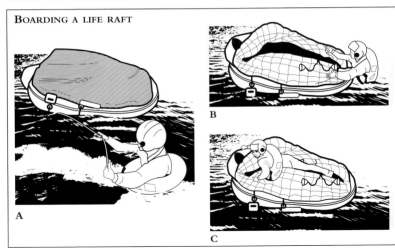

BOARDING A LIFE RAFT

A

B

C

If the raft is attached to you with a rope, pull the raft towards to you (A). If it is upside down in the water, pull it the right way up by moving to the side opposite to where the lanyard is attached and pulling it over, placing your feet against the raft if necessary, or by grabbing handles at the opposite side from where you are in the water and pulling it over.

To board the raft, you can attach your inflatable life-preserver either to yourself or the raft before removing it. Then grab handles on each side of the raft and pull yourself in, while kicking with your legs in the water (B and C). Another way of boarding is to get one knee inside the raft and pull yourself forward into it as shown in D and E.

When you are in the raft, make sure it is fully inflated and check thoroughly for any leaks.

83. SURVIVING IN THE LIFE RAFT

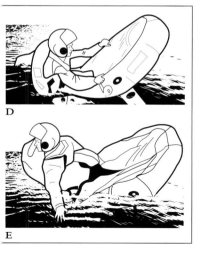

D

E

The immediate priorities are rescue, protection from the elements and water to drink. Observe the following:

- Administer First Aid, giving priority to any wounded survivors.
- Share out dry clothing where possible. Remove wet clothing when appropriate, and dry out. Consider fashioning alternative clothing out of other materials, such as parachute cloth. Those who are wet should be given the most sheltered positions on the raft. Let those who are wet and

cold warm their hands and feet against those who are dry. In a cold climate, huddle together to share warmth. In a hot climate, keep at least one layer of clothing on to protect the body from sunlight.

● Institute water rationing immediately. The rule is that no water is drunk during the first day.

● Check that any signalling equipment is ready to hand, which may include flares, emergency radio and flags. Conserve batteries of signalling equipment – use only when search aircraft or ships are in range.

Use flares only when you are certain that you have been seen. Keep them dry and fire them downwind up and away from the raft.

If the raft is equipped with an Emergency Position Radio Beacon, or EpiRB, attach the antenna and activate, normally by pulling a pin out. There are two kinds of beacon, 406 mhz and 121.5mhz. Both send out a signal that indicates the boat's identification and its position. The 406 sends signals to ships, passing aircraft and satellites, while the 121.5 sends only to ships and aircraft. Most handheld beacons continue to transmit for up to 24 hours. Without a beacon, you could drift at sea for a considerable time without being found.

● Salvage any useful material that may be floating nearby (it can be tied securely to the dinghy to allow more space inside).

● Ensure that one member of the crew is attached to the life raft with a line, in case it tips over and is blown away.

● Check for desalinating equipment and solar stills, and all available supplies of food. Follow life raft instructions, such as inflating the floor, putting out a drogue (sea anchor) to reduce drift, and closing any sea curtains in the direction of the prevailing wind. Paddle towards other dinghies and attach a line of about 8m (26ft).

● Remember to bleed off air if the raft expands in hot weather, and top up the air if the raft contracts in cold weather or at night. Check the

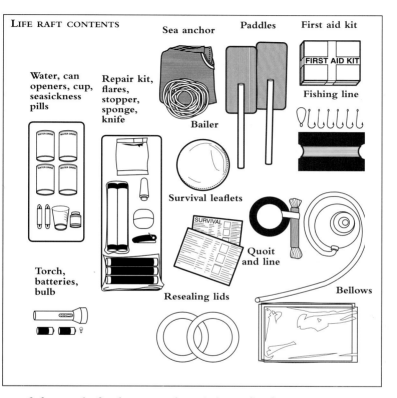

LIFE RAFT CONTENTS

Sea anchor

Paddles

First aid kit

Water, can openers, cup, seasickness pills

Repair kit, flares, stopper, sponge, knife

FIRST AID KIT

Fishing line

Bailer

WATER DRINK   WATER DRINK

WATER DRINK   WATER DRINK

Survival leaflets

SURVIVAL

Quoit and line

Torch, batteries, bulb

Resealing lids

Bellows

raft frequently for damage and repair immediately.

- Bail out water and use any available material to insulate the floor.
- Exercise fingers, toes, legs, arms, buttocks and shoulders frequently to prevent cramps. Keep hands under your armpits.
- Relax and try to keep your mind occupied. Dwelling on your predicament will only make it seem worse.

HUDDLING FOR WARMTH

HELP POSTURE

84. PICKING UP OTHER SURVIVORS

If you are in a life raft and see others in the water, you will need to bring them onboard quickly and without panic:

● Firstly, try to throw them a line with a life belt attached to the end.
● If they are too far away, send a swimmer out attached to a line.
● Approach survivors from behind to avoid them grabbing you around the neck. Grab the back of their life jacket if they have one, or put your hand under their chin and using a sidestroke swim back to the raft.
● Give them reassurance all the time and do not underestimate the strength of a person in a state of panic!

85. SURVIVING IN THE WATER

If no life rafts are available, you have no choice but to go overboard into the water. Do not jump into the water wearing an inflated life jacket — this can cause serious injury.

Once in the water, you may safely inflate your life jacket (if you have one).

Swim steadily and look out for any floating objects, such as pieces of wood, which will help you to keep afloat. If you are escaping from a ditched aircraft, swim or paddle upwind, especially if the plane is on fire. Remember, any large object, such as a plane or boat, will create a suction when it sinks beneath the surface, which can drag survivors down. Therefore, get away from the plane or boat as soon as possible.

If there is burning oil on the water, attempt to swim under it, using underwater breaststroke (you may need to deflate or discard your life jacket). When you need to come up for air, allow enough time to clear a space in the burning area by pushing the water aside from beneath the surface. Then take in enough breath and, if possible, look to check the shortest route to clear water before submerging again, straight downwards, feet first.

Once clear of immediate danger, practise relaxing by floating on your back with your face above the water. This will allow you to recoup energy before swimming again to the nearest life raft or large floating object.

If no life raft is available, but you are wearing a life-jacket, adopt the Heat Escaping Lessening Posture (HELP) to conserve as much body warmth as possible. The principle of HELP is keeping the head clear of the water, since most heat is lost through the head and neck. A towel wrapped round the neck will also prevent heat loss. If there are several of you in the water, huddle close together to preserve body heat. Both of these methods will increase your survival time in the water.

If you have no buoyancy equipment, you can save energy by relaxing into a crouching position, which will allow your body to float just below the surface of the water, and then move your arms to bring your head up to the surface to breathe before relaxing into the crouch again.

You can also enhance your buoyancy by taking off clothing and using it to create a flotation device. Allow as much air as possible inside the sleeves or legs, and tie the ends to seal them. You will need to repeat the procedure periodically, as the air is likely to escape gradually.

86. STACK THE ODDS IN YOUR FAVOUR

The priority is to be seen or find safety such as a landfall. Your chances of being found are greatest if you are close to the area where rescuers were last in radio contact. Stay in the area for at least 72 hours to give them a chance to locate you. To maximize your chances of being rescued:

- Put out a sea anchor in order to stay close to the site. When open, the anchor will help to keep the dinghy in one vicinity. When closed, it will cause the life raft to be pulled along by the current.
- Put up any permanent signals, such as a flag, and work out the best way of using the signalling equipment available in the life raft, following instructions.
- Signalling and navigation equipment should be carefully protected from the elements, but easily accessible if they need to be used quickly.
- Exercise leadership skills where necessary and allocate tasks (such as signaller, navigator, spotter and fisherman). Try to find out who has any specialist skills that might be useful. If you are not the leader, concentrate on carrying out your particular duty effectively and consider the best ways you can do so. Do not interfere with other people's tasks unless asked.
- You will be thinking most clearly in the early stages when you are reasonably well fed and watered, so make plans then that you can remember and follow if things become difficult and you become weaker.
- Keep a log, which records the prevailing winds, weather, currents and state of the crew on board. This will help in such matters as navigation.

87. FINDING WATER AT SEA

The minimum requirement is 500ml (18fl oz) a day, though, in some circumstances, a man or woman can live for up to 10 days without water.

- Do not drink for the first 24 hours, or until you have a headache.
- Drink in a steady way to avoid vomiting. Allow the body to absorb the water rather than over-filling your stomach. Moisten your lips and mouth before swallowing water.
- Do not be tempted to use seawater for drinking or for mixing with fresh water. It is likely to cause vomiting. Alcohol will also exacerbate the water deficiency, so resist the temptation to drink it.
- If there is insufficient water, do not eat, because the food will absorb water from your body. In a hot climate especially, food is secondary.
- Keep physical exertion to a minimum, especially in the hottest parts of the day. Should you feel at all seasick, take whatever seasickness tablets are available. Being sick will result in a heavy loss of water.
- In a hot climate, keep out of direct sunlight and dampen clothes during the day to keep cool, but do not soak. Do not get water in the raft.
- Look out for rain and make sure you catch it in a tarpaulin and/or other containers. Store as much as possible.

SOLAR STILL

A life raft may be supplied with a solar still. Read the instructions carefully, as the still will not work unless the sea is relatively calm.

ICEBERGS

Old sea ice will have lost much of its saltiness, but new ice will be unpalatable. Old ice can be recognized by its smooth shapes and blue tinge. Snow on the surface of sea ice will be fresh. Do not approach any iceberg that looks unstable. Icebergs can roll over at any time without warning! Do not climb onto them for an overnight stay!

88. FINDING FOOD AT SEA

Eat nothing for as long as possible. Carbohydrate-rich foods, such as chocolate and sweets, if available, may be eaten to offset hunger when water is scarce.

CATCHING FISH

Fish are an obvious source of food, but remember not to eat too much with little water. Fish are high in protein, which requires a comparatively larger amount of body water to digest. Offshore fish are usually safe to eat, whereas inshore fish can be poisonous.

Always protect your hands whether holding a fish or a fishing line. Use small fish as bait (rig up a net to catch them); they can also be used as food. Head for large shoals of fish. Cut loose any over-large fish and do not fish if sharks may be near. Take care not to puncture the dinghy with fish hooks.

Fish should be gutted immediately after catching them. Any fish that you will not be eating immediately can be dried in the sun. But do make sure that you have enough water if you are going to eat dried fish.

In addition to a fishing line, you can also bind a knife to an oar to use as a spear to catch larger fish. Be cautious, however, with regard to the size of the dinghy and a be aware of a possible capsize or other damage.

BIRDS

All sea birds are edible. To catch them, use a diamond-shaped gorge, covered in fish; this can be trailed behind the boat and will get stuck in their throat. Alternatively, use a noose, similarly camouflaged, with which you may be able to trap their legs.

SEAWEED

This should be eaten only if it is firm to the touch and odourless. Do not eat slender, branched varieties of seaweed, as they contain irritant acids. Make sure any small sea organisms that may be attached to the seaweed come off before eating. Remember that seaweed is high in protein, requiring a large amount of body water to digest.

89. DANGEROUS SEA LIFE

SHARKS

Some sharks are deadly. Beware of all sharks and try to ensure that you do not draw their attention. Sharks can be found in every ocean and sea, and can sense movement as well as blood and decaying matter, such as vomit.

- Treat seasickness as soon as possible to avoid putting vomit in the water. If you do need to get rid of vomit, throw it as far away as possible behind the raft, so that the current sweeps it away.
- Try to limit the amount of urine or faeces that goes into the water at any one time. If you are cut or have been bitten, stem the bleeding as soon as possible.
- On a dinghy or raft, do not dangle your limbs under the water, and be cautious about underwater repairs of the craft.
- Like most predators, sharks will normally attack an animal that is showing signals of weakness. So if under attack, you may be able to persuade it to turn elsewhere by shouting, slapping the water, kicking or rapping or poking the shark with a stick.

If there are other people in the water, huddle together facing outwards, and beat the water with strong regular strokes. The shark will sense the confidence of the movements.

Let your adrenaline fuel your anger and not your fear.

AUGER OR TENEBRA SHELL

Dangerously poisonous. Similar to cone shells, though narrower and with a less potent poison.

BARRACUDA

Potentially dangerous. A long fish with a protruding jaw, rather like a large pike. Found in the Atlantic, Indian and Pacific oceans. Length of the great barracuda: up to 1.8m (6ft). Barracuda do not normally attack humans.

BLUE-RINGED OCTOPUS
Deadly poisonous. Found mostly in the Australian barrier reef, they can be greyish–white with blue, ringlike marks. Note that all octopuses can vary their colour, so treat any tropical species with caution. The bite can be lethal.

CONE SHELL
Deadly poisonous. Mainly found in tropical regions, these cones have a small opening at the narrow end, from which the animal can shoot out a poisonous needle that is potentially lethal.

PORCUPINE FISH
Poisonous. Greenish with dark patches on the back, with spiny appearance over upper body and sides. Inflates into a ball when alarmed.

PORTUGUESE MAN-OF-WAR
Found mainly in tropical seas, but can drift across to European waters. Floating portion can be as small as 15cm (6in), but tentacles can be 12m (40ft) long. The sting is painful, though not usually fatal.

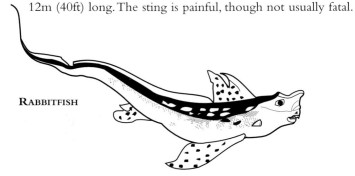

RABBITFISH

PUFFER FISH

Poisonous. Mottled green with black spots. Inflates into a ball when alarmed.

RABBITFISH

Dangerously poisonous. Mottled green, round, flattened shape, with sharp spines on their fins. Length: about 30cm (12in). Although this fish is edible, the spines can cause intense pain.

ROCKFISH, SCORPIONFISH, LIONFISH

Dangerously poisonous. Found in the reefs of the Pacific and Indian oceans. Perchlike fish with large spiny heads.

STINGRAY

Dangerously poisonous. Found usually in warm, shallow water, but also in temperate waters during warm seasons. They have a dark, diamond-shape appearance with a long, whiplike tail. The tail can inflict a serious wound. Stingrays are the most common cause of severe fish stings.

STONEFISH

Deadly poisonous. Found in the shallow waters of the Pacific and Indian oceans. They live among rocks and coral, and in mud flats and estuaries. Because of their mottled green colour, they are very difficult to see. If stepped on, they can inflict an intensely painful, and sometimes fatal, sting.

TENEBRA SHELL

SWORDFISH, MARLIN, SAILFISH, SPEARFISH

These are all large fish with a spike or spear on the upper jaw. These fish are not normally dangerous, but will react if attacked or wounded. Leave them alone, as the spike could be lethal in a life raft. Wounded swordfish have even been known to attack wooden boats.

TANG OR SURGEONFISH

Dangerously poisonous. Tropical water fish with bright blue and green colours. Flat and rounded. Do not be fooled by the pleasant appearance of this fish, as the spines, especially in the tail, can inflict a painful sting.

TOADFISH

Dangerously poisonous. It looks like a cross between a toad and a fish, and lurks in mud in the winter. They can also be found in both shallow and deep water. Sharp spines near the gills and first dorsal fin can inflict a painful sting.

TRIGGERFISH

Poisonous. Can be dark with algae-like greenish patches on the side and underbelly, and stout dorsal spines.

TUNA

Potentially dangerous. A large tuna fish can bite the head off a dolphin. If you are in a small craft, treat them with caution, even though they are good to eat.

WEEVERFISH

Dangerously poisonous. Long-bodied fish (about 30cm/12in) that tend to bury themselves in sand. Their mouths are large and upwardly slanted, with eyes on the top of their heads. They have poisonous spines in the fins, which deliver a painful sting.

In general, be careful of fish that inhabit lagoons and reefs, and in particular of fish with small, parrot-like mouths and small belly fins.

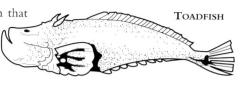

TOADFISH

90. HOW TO TREAT POISONS INJECTED BY FISH SPINES

Immediately wash the wound thoroughly with water. Then take a sharp knife, make a small cut across the wound and apply suction. If you do not have a knife, apply suction anyway to remove as much venom as possible.

Suck out as much of the poison as possible, spit it out and immerse the injured part in hot water (as hot as you can bear) for 30–60 minutes. Should the wound be to the face, use a hot compress.

Clean the wound and cover with antiseptic and a sterile dressing, and if necessary treat casualty for any shock.

91. NAVIGATING AT SEA

If you are in a properly equipped life raft, it should contain navigation equipment with instructions. If you do not have the usual equipment, such as a compass or sextant, the following points may help:

SUNRISE METHOD

The sun rises in the east and sets in the west. If you are north of latitude 23.5°N, the sun will pass south of you. If you are south of latitude 23.5°S, the sun will pass north of you. If you are between these two latitudes, the sun's path varies according to the time of year.

Use the table overleaf to estimate your position according to the direction in which the sun rises at certain times of year.

SUNRISE TABLE

LATITUDE	60°NORTH	30°NORTH	0°EQUATOR	30°SOUTH
21 Mar	89	90	90	90
5 May	55	71	74	72
22 Jun	37	63	67	64
9 Aug	55	71	74	72
23 Sep	89	90	90	90
7 Nov	122	108	106	104
22 Dec	140	116	113	117
5 Feb	122	108	106	109

WATCH METHOD

Between sunrise and sunset, and north and south of the latitudes shown in the table (N at 60° and S at 30° S), you can gain a rough estimate of direction by using your watch. Aim the hour hand at the sun. The point half way between the hour hand and twelve o'clock will show the approximate direction of true south if you are in the northern hemisphere, and the approximate direction of true north if you are in the southern hemisphere.

However, if you are in the tropics, (that is, between 23.5°N and 23.5°S), this method is unreliable.

STARS

The night stars are a reliable guide and have been used by navigators for thousands of years.

The key navigational aid in the northern hemisphere is Polaris (North Star), which stands over the North Pole. Polaris is part of a faint constellation known as Ursa Minor (Little Bear), or Little Dipper, and can be identified in the sky by following a line through the two brightest stars of the constellation known as Ursa Major (Great Bear), or Big Dipper. Without a sextant and navigation tables, you will be able to get only a very approximate idea of your latitude by measuring the angle of the North Star over the horizon. A five-degree margin of error in the angle could put you out by 300 nautical miles.

In the southern hemisphere, the Southern Cross is used as a guide. The four brightest stars form a cross tilting to the side. Follow the axis of the two furthest apart and continue an imaginary line five times the length of this axis. At the point where this imaginary line ends, you will find south.

92. WEATHER AT SEA

Sailors are acutely aware of signs that indicate which way the weather is likely to turn. Two good indicators are the wind and the clouds. By recognizing the direction and changes of wind, the types of cloud and the likely weather they indicate, you can prepare better for either good or bad weather.

WINDS

At low levels, winds flow around regions of relatively low pressure (cyclones) and high pressure (anti-cyclones). Winds flow anticlockwise around lows in the northern hemisphere, and clockwise in the southern hemisphere. Wind systems rotate in the opposite direction around the centres of high pressure.

Lying approximately between latitudes 10°S and 10°N is an area of low pressure and hot air. This area is known as the Doldrums. On the edge of the Doldrums, winds rise to create towering cumulonimbus clouds and heavy rain. At latitudes 30°N and 30°S from the equator, there are high-pressure belts of light, variable winds. The air moving from these latitudes towards the Doldrums is known as the trade winds, or the prevailing winds in the lower latitudes.

In the northern hemisphere, the prevailing wind that flows from the north, southwards to the equator is called the north-east trade wind. It is not a straight north–south flow because of deflection by the rotation of the earth. The corresponding wind in the southern hemisphere is called the south-east trade wind.

In the middle latitudes, the winds are called the prevailing westerlies, though their direction can be affected daily by a number of factors. During the summer, the continents are areas of low pressure, attracting winds in from the colder oceans. In the winter, the continents have high pressure, and winds flow towards the warmer oceans.

LOCAL WINDS

In the summer, in particular, the land is warmer than the sea during the day, but it is colder than the sea at night. Breezes thus flow from the sea into the land during the day, and flow out from the land towards the sea at night. This phenomenon occurs across a band of up to 50km (31 miles) width, over land and sea.

OCEAN CURRENTS

The prevailing winds (which are seen in the map overleaf) affect the ocean currents.

THE BEAUFORT SCALE

DESCRIPTION & WIND SPEED (KNOTS)
0 Calm (less than 1)
1 Light air (1–3)
2 Light breeze (4–6)
3 Gentle breeze (7–10)
4 Moderate breeze (11–16)
5 Fresh breeze (17–21)
6 Strong breeze (22–27)
7 Near gale (28–33)
8 Gale (34–40)
9 Strong gale (41–47)
10+ Storm (48+)

LAND SIGNS	SEA SIGNS
Smoke rises vertically. Leaves do not stir.	
Smoke drifts. Wind vanes are still.	
Wind on face. Rustling leaves. Vanes move.	
Light flags extended. Leaves in motion.	Small waves (average wave height 0.6m/2ft)
Small branches moving. Dust raised.	Small waves, some with white crests (average wave height 1m/3ft 3ins) height
Small trees sway. Tops of trees move.	White horses and spray off tops of waves (average wave height 1.8m/6ft)
Large branches in motion. Whistling wires.	
Trees in motion. Walkers buffeted.	Seas piling up. Foam (average wave height 13ft/4m)
Twigs broken off trees. Difficult to walk.	
Chimney pots and slates fall.	Waves high with dense foam (average wave height 7m/23ft)
Trees uprooted.	Very high waves, large expanses of froth, edges of all waves turned to foam (average wave height 11.3m/37ft)

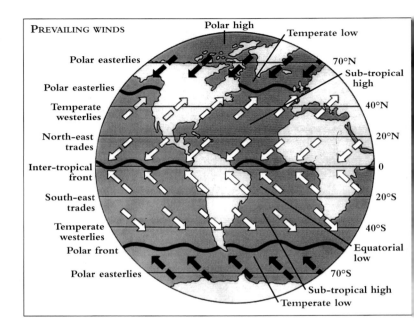

PREVAILING WINDS

Polar high

Temperate low

Polar easterlies

70°N

Sub-tropical high

Polar easterlies

Temperate westerlies

40°N

North-east trades

20°N

Inter-tropical front

0

South-east trades

20°S

Temperate westerlies

40°S

Polar front

Equatorial low

Polar easterlies

70°S

Sub-tropical high

Temperate low

CLOUDS

Four main groups of clouds are categorized on the basis of height above the earth.

CIRRUS

Usually about 6km (3¾ miles) above the earth, Cirrus clouds are composed of ice particles. They are feathery and elongated, and appear as bands. They are known as mare's tails. These clouds can often indicate fine weather, but when they are accompanied by a regular north wind in cold climates, they sometimes precede a blizzard.

- **Cirrostratus**
  This consists of a fine veil of whitish clouds, darker than cirrus. When cirrostratus follows cirrus across the sky, bad weather may be due.

- **Cirrocumulus**
  Small white balls arranged in groups, these clouds indicate good weather.

CUMULUS

Fluffy, white and heaped together, these clouds are often indicators of fine weather, and can appear around midday on a sunny day. If they pile up and push higher into the atmosphere, they can become storm clouds.

NIMBUS

Clouds of uniform greyness extend over the whole sky.

- **Cumulonimbus**
  Towering into the atmosphere, these clouds are dark with flat bases and rounded tops. Sometimes they form an anvil shape at the top, looking like cirrus. They often mean sudden heavy showers of rain, snow or hail. If a thunderstorm occurs, you can expect a strong wind from the direction of the storm as well as a rapid drop in temperature.

STRATUS

Low clouds composed of water droplets make up an even, grey layer of cloud. They inevitably mean rain or snow.

- **Altostratus**
  Holes in this layer mean that the weather may not be too bad.

- **Nimbostratus**
  These rain-bearing clouds have a low base and consist of thick layers.

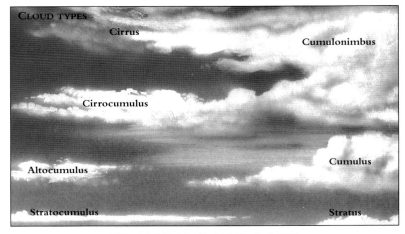

93. HOW TO FIND LAND

If rescue has not come or if, for any reason, you consider this to be unlikely (you may be too far out to sea), then attempting to move towards land may be advisable.

The life raft will be moved by a mixture of water current and wind. If the raft is low in the water, the effect of the current will be maximized. If it is high in the water and travelling light, the wind effect will be proportionately greater. Assess which is the most efficient way of making progress. If there is a high wind, it is probably a good idea to bring in the drogue (sea anchor) and throw out unnecessary ballast.

INDICATIONS OF LAND

A stationary cumulus cloud is often an indication of the presence of an island, and a lagoon can create a greenish reflection on the underside of clouds.

Birds will often be heading towards land in the afternoon and evening. Look out for the particular types of bird and the direction they are flying. In the morning, they will probably be heading away from land.

Floating vegetation and pieces of timber may indicate the proximity of land.

An excerpt from *The Kon-Tiki Expedition*, by Thor Heyerdahl, illustrates the possibilities of finding land:

'With each day that passed, larger flocks of sea birds came and circled over us aimlessly in all directions. One evening, when the sun was about to sink into the sea, we perceived clearly that the birds had received a violent impetus. They were flying away in a westerly direction without paying any attention to us or the flying fish beneath them. And from the masthead we could see that as they came over they all flew straight on exactly the same course. Perhaps they saw something from up above which we did not see. Perhaps they were flying by instinct. In any case they were flying with a plan, straight home to the nearest island, their breeding-place.

'We twisted the steering oar and set our course exactly in the direction in which the birds had disappeared. Even after it was dark we heard the cries of stragglers flying over us against the starry sky on exactly the same course as that which we were now following. It was a wonderful night; the moon was nearly full for the third time in the course of the Kon-Tiki's voyage.

'Next day there were still more birds over us, but we did not need to wait for them to show us our way again in the evening. This time we had detected a curious stationary cloud above the horizon. The lonely cloud on the horizon to the south-west did not move; it just rose like a motionless column of smoke while the trade wind clouds drifted by. Cumulonimbus is the Latin name for such clouds. The Polynesians did not know this, but they did know that under such clouds land lay. For when the tropical sun bakes the hot sand, a stream of warm air is created which rises up and causes its vapour content to condense up in the colder strata of air.'

(Chapter VI, Across the Pacific II)

94. HOW TO MAKE LANDFALL

Signal if the land is likely to be inhabited and wait for rescuers to come out to you. If you have to make a landing, choose your position carefully, keeping clear of rocks or strong surf. Look for gaps in the surf line. Go round to the lee of the island, where you will be sheltered from the wind. Strong tidal currents may wash you back out to sea, so try to spot a sloping beach where the surf is less strong.

You may be carried along parallel to the beach and some distance out to sea by a rip current, or rip tide. This is a surge of excess sea water escaping from the beach. Do not try to swim or paddle directly against the current. Swim or paddle along with the rip current for a short distance to allow its force to dissipate. Then head back in towards the shore.

Beware of coral reefs in the Pacific – they will be difficult to see from low down in the water. Keep looking out for gaps. Do not get so close that you are sucked on to the reef. If you are negotiating a reef in a raft or dinghy, put out the sea anchor to pull the craft head on to the obstacle. Pull the sea anchor in when you judge the moment is right to take a wave over the reef. Wear shoes and hang on to the craft when going over coral or rocks. When coming in to beach, ride the crest of a large wave and remain in the craft until it is grounded.

Again in *The Kon-Tiki Expedition*, Thor Heyerdahl wrote:

'We tied the longest rope we had to the home-made anchor and made it fast to the step of the port mast, so that the Kon-Tiki would go into the surf stern first when the anchor was thrown overboard. The anchor itself consisted of empty water cans filled with used wireless batteries and heavy scrap, and solid mangrove-wood sticks projected from it, set crosswise.

'Order number one, which came first and last, was: Hold on to the raft! Whatever happened we must hang on tight on board and let the nine great logs take the pressure from the reef. We ourselves had more than enough to do to withstand the weight of the water.'

(Chapter VII, To the South Sea Islands)

If you have to swim ashore, keep your clothing on and sit in the water with your feet up as protection against rock.

95. BUILDING YOUR OWN RAFT

Once on land, you may decide to build your own raft (see also Tip 107). Use trees and driftwood found along the shore. Knowing how to lash logs together properly could save your life. The wider the raft, the more stable it will be when people are sitting on it.

Rafts are good for river travel, and hopping between islands, but not recommended for long sea crossings unless you have no choice. Test the raft thoroughly in safe shallow water before setting out and tie all equipment securely to the raft.

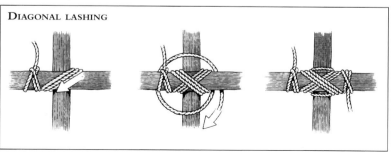

DIAGONAL LASHING

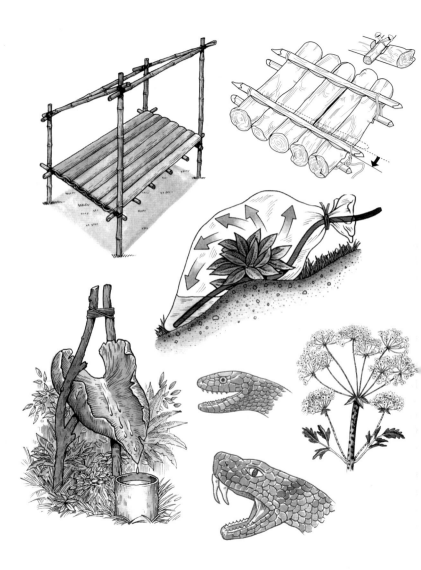

SURVIVING IN THE TROPICS

The tropics present hazards in the form of infested swamps, bushfire, poisonous plants and deadly wildlife, but they are rich in nutritious vegetation, hidden sources of water and possibilities for shelter. Most people think of tropical regions in terms of thick jungle, infested by every kind of danger imaginable. But this is far from the truth, as there are different kinds of tropical climate, most of which contain plenty of water and plant and animal food.

There are five kinds of tropical climates: rain forests, semi-evergreen, tropical scrub, seasonal forests and tropical savannas. In survival situations, the tropical jungle can provide all things to maintain life.

RAIN FOREST

More than 180cm (72cm) of annual precipitation and a hot, steamy climate are the conditions of a tropical rain forest, which produces the most diverse vegetation types in the world. Typical rain forests are found in South and Central America, West and Central Africa, Indonesia, parts of Southeast Asia, and in tropical Australia.

Temperatures are both even and high, with mean monthly temperatures between 24°C (75°F) and 28°C (82°F). This is because the upper layers of tree canopies and lower layers of branches filter sunlight and reduce wind movement. The forest normally has three layers of tree crowns: the highest forms the forest canopy; below this is a layer of young trees, shrubs, large herbs and lianas; and a third layer, of tree branches, twigs and foliage, lies just above ground level. The forest floor is relatively clear, with a layer of humus and fallen leaves. Humidity is very high near the forest floor, but more variable near the canopy.

There are mountainous regions in all major areas of rain forest and increases in altitude are matched by increases in rainfall.

PRIMARY AND SECONDARY JUNGLE

Primary jungle is typified by a combination of tall trees and layers of vegetation below, as described above. Secondary jungle results from the clearance of primary jungle for cultivation by man. The jungle eventually reclaims an abandoned cultivated area, but instead of tall trees there is a mixture of dense undergrowth and creepers, making this kind of jungle more difficult to cross.

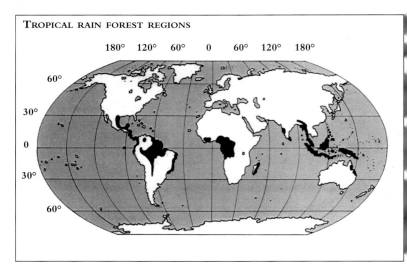

TROPICAL RAIN FOREST REGIONS

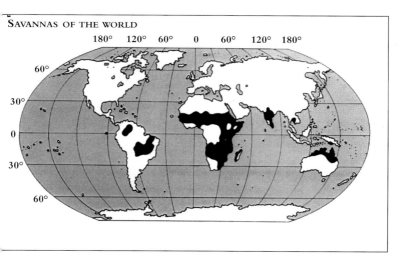

SAVANNAS OF THE WORLD

MONSOON FOREST

Also called dry, or tropical deciduous, forest, the monsoon forest has trees that shed their leaves in the dry season. This type of forest is most evident in Southeast Asia and is characterized by teak trees and bamboo thickets.

SAVANNA

Savanna is found in tropical regions around 8° to 20° from the equator. Mean annual precipitation is somewhere in the region of 80–150cm (32–60in), and rain falls from about October to March in the southern hemisphere and April to September in the northern. Mean monthly temperatures are between 10°C (50°F) and 20°C (68°F) in the dry season; 20°C (68°F) and 30°C (86°F) in the wet season.

Savanna is characterized by continuous grass cover, but it can vary according to the density of trees and shrubs. There are categories of woodland, tree, shrub and grass savanna. Bushfires are common in the dry season, and are influenced by human activity.

MANGROVE SWAMPS

Mangroves develop in both tropical and sub-tropical regions, and can be found in the river deltas of the Amazon, Mekong, Congo, and Ganges. Many of the animals that populate these areas are dangerous or unpleasant, such as leeches, stinging insects, crocodiles and caimans.

FRESHWATER SWAMPS

Found inland, freshwater swamps are mostly near rivers that supply the water for them. The water flows slowly through the abundant vegetation, and these areas are difficult to navigate. Tropical swamps include sedges, such as papyrus, as well as trees such as palms.

96. TRAVELLING THROUGH JUNGLE COUNTRY

Ideally, to be rescued, you should stay in one place. However, the dense jungle canopy will make it difficult for any rescuers in planes or helicopters to locate you. So, although you may be severely restricted by dense vegetation, travel may be the only realistic way of being found. Owing to the number of obstacles and potential danger from animals, travel in the jungle must be undertaken with great care and planning:

- First of all, try to pinpoint your present location. If you land in the jungle by parachute, make a note of rivers and other landmarks before you enter the tree cover.
- Use your compass to set a course and follow it as closely as possible, bearing in mind that although any jungle tracks that you encounter may not be on your course, they will be much easier to follow than hacking through dense bush. Take a bearing on a landmark that you can keep in

sight, and then choose another one after it, and so on.

- If you wish to be able to return to your original location for any reason, mark your trail by leaving cuts in trees or piles of upturned leaves or stones.
- To find human habitation, you will need to follow the course of a river or stream. Native villages are normally sited on the banks or confluence of rivers. Bear in mind that trails and rivers will often be used by animals at night, many of which will be dangerous.
- Dead or decaying vegetation may mean danger from falling branches, so keep clear of it if possible.
- Steer clear of swamps, as it will be almost impossible to make headway. They are also likely to contain dangerous animals.
- Never cross a river with a rucksack fully strapped to your back.
- Attention needs to be given regularly to leeches, chiggers and other parasites, which should be cleared from boots, clothing and skin.
- Attend to bites or scratches, which quickly turn septic in the jungle. For this reason, shaving, although a morale booster in many circumstances, is not a good idea.
- Only move through the jungle in daylight.
- Move slowly through thick vegetation. Use a stick to part undergrowth; this will avoid disturbing ant and scorpion nests with your hands or feet. Do not hold onto vines when crossing slopes – the thorns and spines will cause irritation and they may not hold your weight!

97. CLOTHING FOR THE TROPICS

An environment with close, often thorny, vegetation and a vast range of insects as well as leeches, demands strong clothing and is not a place for the scantily clad. Thick trousers and strong shirts are recommended, as well as plenty of clean changes of socks. Weight considerations may mean it is not possible to take more than two changes of clothing (not including socks).

If so, keep one dry set sealed up in waterproof bags to change into at the end of journeys and for night wear. Due to the humidity, clothes are unlikely to dry quickly, so it is better to change back into the wet kit for the next journey.

It is crucially important to check footwear and other clothing for insects before putting them on. Powder your body with zinc talcum powder and use insect repellent on your body and socks to keep leeches, mosquitoes and a host of other undesirable creatures at bay.

98. HOW TO BUILD PROTECTIVE SHELTER

In tropical regions, it is important to be aware of the possibility of flooding, so find high ground and/or an area where there is no evidence of previous flooding, such as silt. Make sure there is no dead wood above or immediately around you, as this could fall in a storm and cause severe injury. Termites are one sign of dead wood. Also keep away from coconuts or any other large objects that may fall. Clear away dead and rotting vegetation from around your campsite. This will allow your fire ventilation reduce hiding places for snakes and insects, and also make you more visible to rescue aircraft. Do not camp close to streams during the rainy season: flash floods can occur without warning.

HAMMOCK
A hammock is ideal in tropical regions, as it keeps you away from potential flooding and from insects on the ground. Either carry a specialist hammock with mosquito netting or improvise a hammock by making use of a parachute.

A-FRAME WITH THATCHED LEAVES
Construct an A-type framework and cover it with overlapping layers of banana, atap or other broad leaves.

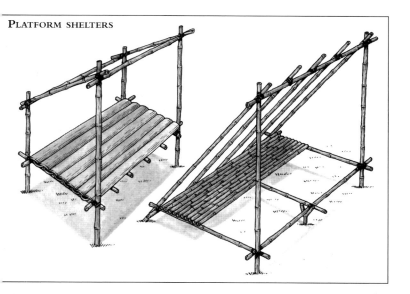

PLATFORM SHELTERS

PLATFORM SHELTERS

These can be made from wood or bamboo lashed together. Bamboo can be split down the sides to create interlocking sections to be used as a bed and/or a roof. Large leaves, such as palm and atap, can be woven together to create a roof and walls for the shelter and also bedding. Take care when handling bamboo, as it can split suddenly when cut and send out sharp splinters. Leaves can be razor sharp and can inflict painful cuts if not handled carefully.

SWAMP BED

The purpose of this is to keep you safe in a swamp. Either find four trees in a rectangle or drive four poles into the ground. Lash some cross poles across at both ends. Poles should then be laid along the long sides, resting on top of the crosswise short poles. Place cross bars all the way along the length of the swamp bed. On top of this, you can lay leaves and/or grass for a softer sleeping base. Make sure that the bed is large enough for both yourself and your equipment.

99. FINDING WATER

Although the tropical survivor is not likely to have the same difficulty as the desert survivor in finding sources of water, the problems should not be underestimated.

- To locate water, look out for signs of bees, ants or flies, which all need water and may lead you directly to a source.
- Some birds, such as finches and pigeons, are good indicators of a water source. When they are flying fast and low, they are likely to be heading towards water. When they pause frequently for rest, they are likely to be coming away from water.
- Avoid discoloured water and water that smells bad. Avoid water that has foam or bubbles in it, and water with a lack of healthy green vegetation growing around it.

STREAMS

If the stream is fast-flowing with a stone and sand bed, the water is likely to be pure, although it is not always possible to ascertain whether there are animal deposits farther upstream.

Boil or purify the water if you are in any doubt. In any case, do not drink directly from the surface, but use a receptacle to check that the water is free from such things as leeches.

Muddy water can be strained through a sand-filled cloth or a bamboo pipe filled with leaves and/or grass.

MAKING A RAIN TRAP

Set a rain trap by using large leaves positioned to funnel rainwater into a container.

COLLECTING DEW

Tie rags round your ankles and walk through dew-covered grass before sunrise. The rags will become impregnated with water, which you can then wring out into a receptacle.

Tie a rag round a slanted tree, leaving one end loose. The water will drip down the rag into a receptacle on the ground.

MAKING WATER SAFE TO DRINK

The best way of purifying water is to boil it for at least three minutes

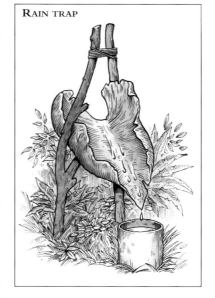

RAIN TRAP

or to use water-sterilizing tablets. Alternatively, use two or three drops of iodine to 1 litre (1¾ pints) of water, and leave to stand for 30 minutes; use a few grains of permanganate of potash (a form of salt derived from permanganic acid) to 1 litre (1¾ pints) of water and allow to stand for 30 minutes.

The following sources of water will most probably require purification:

Stagnant water, such as small pools or water in tree trunks.
Water holes and large rivers.
In both cases, the water should be strained, allowed to stand for a few hours, strained again, then purified by boiling or with sterilizing tablets.

● Water from digging. Dig into sand a few yards from the seashore and stop digging as soon as water starts collecting. The water should be fairly clean and free from salt.

100. GETTING WATER FROM PLANTS

BAMBOO
Sometimes you can find water in the base of large bamboo stems.

GREEN BAMBOO
Bend a piece of bamboo and tie it down. Cut off the top and let the water drip into a receptacle overnight.

BAMBOO

COCONUTS
Green, unripe coconuts have refreshing milk, which is a good substitute for fresh water. Do no drink from ripe and faller coconuts.

BANANA OR PLANTAIN TREE STUMP
Cut the tree, leaving about a 60cm (2ft) stump. Scoop out the stump leaving a bowl-shaped hollow. Water will begin to flow into the bowl from the roots.

VINE
Cut a lower portion of vine about 1.2m (4ft) in length and catch the liquid that drips out. If the liquid is

milky, do not drink it. If it is clear, it may be drinkable: let the liquid flow out and watch to see that it does not change colour. If it tastes like water or has a sweet or woody taste, it should be safe to drink. If the liquid is sour or bitter to taste, avoid it.

LARGE-LEAVED PLANTS

In the tropics, plants with large leaves, such as pitcher plants, will catch rain water. Make sure the water is properly strained to extract insects.

VEGETATION STILLS

Tie a translucent plastic bag round a branch so that it covers the foliage at the end. Weigh or tie down the branch so that transpiration water from it can drip into the bag. It takes a long time to collect water from vegeta-

VEGETATION BAG

tion, so you must set up several stills. Water collected in this way tastes foul, but will keep you alive!

VEGETATION BAG
Place vegetation in a bag and leave it in the sun so that the heat extracts the moisture in the foliage.

101. FINDING FOOD

Food, ranging from banana plants to coconuts and mango, is abundant in the tropics, but the usual care should be taken with potentially poisonous plants like the castor bean.

EDIBLE PLANTS

Bael fruit
Found in India and Burma and other tropical rain forests. The fruit grows on a tree about 2.5–5m (8–16ft) tall, and is grey or yellow and contains seeds.

Bamboo
Although native to the Far East, these plants can be found in many parts of the world. The appearance will be familiar and the young shoots, up to about 30cm (12in) in height can be eaten raw. The fine black hairs along the edge of the leaves of the young shoot are poisonous and should be removed. You can also eat the bamboo seeds when boiled. Bamboo provides all sorts of uses as shelter frames, water carriers, utensils and tools.

Banana and plantain
Found widely in the humid tropics. These tree-like plants have large leaves, and the flowers hang in clusters. You can eat the fruit either raw or cooked.

SURVIVING IN THE TROPICS

The flowers, rootstocks and leaf sheaths of many species can be boiled and eaten. The centre can also be eaten either cooked or raw.

Bignay
Found wild, from the Himalayas through Sri Lanka, South-East Asia and northern Australia. Bignay is a shiny, evergreen shrub with currant-like, red or black fruit. It can be eaten raw or jellied.

Breadfruit
Found in the South Pacific, but also the West Indies and Polynesia. A tree with dark green leaves and large, green, round fruit. The fruit can be baked whole on hot embers for about half an hour, or it can be boiled, baked or fried in slices. Its seeds can be boiled or roasted.

COCONUT

Coconut
Coconuts are found throughout the tropics, mostly near coasts. The white meat inside the fruit can be eaten and the liquid in the unripe fruit is a good thirst-quencher. The palm 'cabbage', or sheath from which the leaves protrude, is found at the top of the plant and may be eaten raw, boiled or roasted.

Fishtail palm
Found in India, Burma, Southeast Asia and the Philippines. These tall trees have a large flowering shoot that hangs downwards. The leaves are oval or wedge-shaped, unlike other palms. Juice can be drawn from the palm shoot. The palm cabbage can either be eaten raw or cooked.

Mango
Grown throughout the tropics. The tree has shiny, alternate leaves. The fruit is oval and turns orange when ripe. It is eaten raw.

Manioc
Also known as tapioca or cassava, it is widespread in the tropics. The plant is 1–2m (3–7ft) high with large, tuber-like roots. One type of manioc is sweet, the other bitter. The bitter one contains poisonous hydrocyanic acid. Cook the bitter type, grate or mash the roots into pulp, squeeze out the pulp and cook the remaining dough for at least an hour.

Nipa palm
Found throughout Southeast Asia. The long leaves collect at the base to form what little there is of a trunk. The flower stalk and seeds are a good source of water and food.

Pawpaw
Found in both tropical and some temperate areas. The fruit grows directly from the trunk and tends to turn yellow when ripe. It can be eaten either raw or cooked.

Rattan palm
Found in rain forests in tropical Africa, Asia, the East Indies and Australia, this is a climber with a whitish flower. Eat the stem tips and palm heart roasted or raw.

TARO

Sago palm

Found in Southeast Asia, mainly in swamps and by lakes and rivers. The palm is squat with long, arching leaves. The pith of the tree will provide sago, which can be cooked.

Sugar palm

Found in many parts of the tropics, with very large leaves. The young flower will yield sugar and the seeds can be boiled.

Sweetsop

Widely distributed in tropical regions, this small tree has a bumpy shaped fruit, which can be eaten raw.

Taro

Found widely in the tropics, this plant is about 50–100cm (20–40in) high, and has large heart-shaped leaves. The roots, young leaves and stalks are all edible and should be either boiled or roasted.

Water lily

Found in temperate and subtropical regions in streams and lakes. The seeds and thickened roots of any variety of lily may be eaten boiled or roasted.

Wild yam

Widely distributed in tropical regions, the yam is a ground creeper, and its root can be boiled and eaten like a vegetable.

Wild rice

Found in wet areas in tropical and temperate climates. It is a tall grass, which yields grains that can be collected, threshed and winnowed to remove the husks. The rice can be boiled or roasted and then pounded to make flour.

102. TROPICAL PLANTS TO AVOID

HEMLOCK

CASTOR BEAN

Deadly poisonous. Also known as the castor oil plant. Native to tropical Africa, it is found in all tropical regions, as well as some temperate regions. It grows to about 12m (40ft) with orange, petal-less flowers. The fruit is covered in soft, orange-brown spines. The bean-shaped seeds contain castor oil and are extremely poisonous.

COWHAGE

Dangerously poisonous. Found in the United States and in tropical areas, it has purplish flowers on a vinelike stem, with seeds in brown hairy pods. Skin contact causes irritation, and contact with eyes can cause blindness.

HEMLOCK

Deadly poisonous. Member of the parsley family and found worldwide in grassy wastelands. It is a coarse, unpleasant-smelling plant with hollow purple-spotted stems and dense clusters of small white flowers, white roots and a bad smell.

All parts of the plant are poisonous and may be fatal if eaten. The poisonous principles in hemlock are alkaloids that affect the nervous system and induce trembling, loss of coordination, and paralysis of respiration.

LANTANA

Deadly poisonous. Mostly cultivated as an ornamental plant, it can also be found as a weed in tropical and temperate areas. The flowers can be white, yellow, orange, pink or red, with a dark blue, blackberry-shaped fruit. It causes dermatitis.

MANCHINEEL

Dangerously poisonous. Found in the southern United States, Central America and northern South America, this tree can grow to about 15m (45ft), with shiny green leaves and small, greenish flowers. The fruit is green to yellow when ripe. It causes dermatitis.

PANGI

Dangerously poisonous. Found in Southeast Asia. A tree with heart-shaped leaves and green flowers. It has a large, brown, pear-shaped fruit, which is particularly poisonous.

PHYSIC NUT

Dangerously poisonous. Found in the southern United States and throughout the tropics. A shrub with small, green to yellow flowers and apple-sized fruit.

POISON SUMAS

Dangerously poisonous. Found in swamps in North America. A dark-spotted, smooth-stemmed shrub with green-yellow flowers and white berries. It causes dermatitis.

ROSARY PEA

Deadly poisonous. Found in Africa, southern North America, the Caribbean and Central and South America. A vine with purple flowers and red and black seeds.

STRYCHNINE TREE

Deadly poisonous. Found in Southeast Asia and Australia. An evergreen tree that can be 12m (40ft) high. It has greenish flowers and orange to red berries.

WATER HEMLOCK OR COW BANE

Deadly poisonous. Found near water worldwide, including swamps. It has purple-streaked stems, toothed leaflets with clusters of small white flowers, and a solid turnip-like root.

103. TROPICAL ANIMALS FOR FOOD

Animals in the rain forest tend to be small and tree-living, which can make capturing them difficult. The few larger rain forest animals include the elephant and the okapi, a shy and rarely seen relative of the giraffe.

In Africa, there are two kinds of pig living in the forest: the bush pig, or red river hog, and the giant forest hog. In Asia, there are three kinds of pig: the common wild boar, the bearded pig and the babirussa, which has upward-growing tusks.

In South America, there are two kinds of peccary (piglike animals)   living in the rain forest, though only the white-tailed peccary is a true tropical rain forest dweller. Both kinds of peccaries have musk glands situated on the spine about 10cm (4in) up from the tail. If you intend to eat the animal, these glands must be removed otherwise the flesh will be unfit to eat.

All these animals can be dangerous and, realistically, should be hunted only with a rifle or a good spear.

OTHER ANIMALS OF THE TROPICAL RAIN FOREST

Anoa ox (Sulawesi, Indonesia)	Mouse deer (Asia)
Asian water buffalo	Monkeys and apes
Bushbuck (Africa)	Moon rats (Asia)
Duikers (Africa – incl. Bates'	Pygmy hippopotamus
Pygmy Antelope, Royal Antelope)	

Elephant shrews (Africa)

Forest deer, including sambar, swamp deer, axis deer or chital (Asia)

Tamarau ox (Philippines)

Tapirs (Asia, South America and Malaysia)

Tree kangaroos (Australia and New Guinea)

Rodents (paca and agouti from South America)

Sloths (South America)

Squirrels (Africa and Asia)

Tree shrews (South-East Asia)

Water chevrotain (Africa)

Wild forest ox or gaur (India and Malaysia)

Birds

Birds of paradise (Australia)

Cassowaries (Australia)

Congo peacock (Africa)

Guinea fowl (Africa)

Hornbills (Africa and Asia)

Hummingbirds (South America)

Parrots, including cockatoos, lories and Pygmy parrots (Australia)

Peacock (India and Sri Lanka)

Pheasants, including jungle fowl (Asia)

Pigeon (including crowned pigeon)

Sunbirds (Africa and Asia)

Turacos (Africa)

Toucans (South America)

Woodcreepers (South America)

Invertebrates

Beetles

Butterflies

Centipedes

Millipedes

Spiders

Predators

Himalayan black bear (Himalayas and Indo-China)

Jaguar (South America)

Leopard (Africa and Asia)

Marsupial tiger cat (Australia)

Small to medium-sized cats

Tiger (Asia)

Reptiles and amphibians

Chameleon (Africa and Asia) Gecko (Asia)

Flattened tree snake (Asia) Snakes

Flying frog (Asia) Tree frogs (Africa, Asia,

Flying lizards (Asia) South America)

Birds, lizards and snakes are all edible, though great care should be taken with the latter. Ants, grubs, grasshoppers and crickets are also edible, though wings and legs should first be removed. Grubs can be split and broiled over a fire.

104. POISONOUS SNAKES

The following poisonous snakes are found in the Americas:

BUSHMASTER

Deadly poisonous. Bushmaster is the common name for this venomous snake of the viper family. Found in Central and South America in lowland tropical forests. The bushmaster is the only American pit viper that lays eggs.

Pinkish brown with dark, triangular markings. Length: average 2–2.6m (7–9ft).

CORAL SNAKE

Deadly poisonous. There are around 50 species of coral snake and most of them are found in southern and central America. Distinctly coloured in bands of black, red, yellow and white. Length: average 67cm (27in). Some south American coral snakes reach a length of 2m (about 7ft).

COTTONMOUTH

Dangerously poisonous. Also known as the moccasin or water moccasin.

Lives in the swamps of southern United States and parts of Illinois, Kentucky, Missouri, Oklahoma and Texas. When threatened, it holds its mouth open; it is called the cottonmouth because the lining of its mouth is white. It feeds on fish, amphibians, reptiles, birds and small mammals. Like all vipers, the cottonmouth has hollow fangs that inject toxic venom into its victim. The bite is rarely fatal, although will be painful and can cause local tissue damage.

Coloured brown or olive, with broad black bands across its body. Length: average 90cm (3ft).

EASTERN DIAMONDBACK RATTLESNAKE

Dangerously poisonous. Found in the southern United States in swamps and elsewhere. Also capable of swimming out to sea. Olive or brown colour with dark brown or black diamonds. Length: average 1.5m (5ft).

EYELASH PIT VIPER

Deadly poisonous. Found in southern Mexico, Central America and South America. It lives mostly in trees. Its colour can vary from uniform yellow to reddish-yellow spots. Length: average 45cm (18in).

JUMPING VIPER

Deadly poisonous. The jumping viper is found in southern Mexico and Central America. It is brown or grey with black markings. Length: average 60cm (2ft).

The following poisonous snakes are found in Africa and Asia:

BUSH VIPER

Poisonous. Found in most of Africa. It lives mainly in trees, but hunts on the ground. Colour varies from pale green through olive to reddish brown. Length: average 45cm (18in).

GABOON VIPER

Dangerously poisonous. Found in most of Africa, mainly in dense rain forest. The colour varies from pink to brown with yellow or brown spots on the back. Length: average 1.2m (4ft).

GREEN MAMBA

Deadly poisonous. Found in most parts of tropical and southern Africa, usually in brush and trees. Mambas are among the swiftest snakes on Earth. All have narrow heads with large eyes. Their venom is very potent and will kill a human if not treated with antivenin. The green mamba is uniformly coloured, and the larger black mamba is olive or black. Length: 1.5–2m (5–7ft).

GREEN TREE PIT VIPER

Dangerously poisonous. Found in India and Southeast Asia. The colour is uniformly bright or dull green. Length: average 45cm (18in).

KING COBRA

Deadly poisonous. The king cobra is the world's longest venomous snake. Found in the Philippines, Malaysia, southern China, Burma, India, Thailand and the Malay Peninsula. Its main food is other snakes. In India it is regarded with religious awe and therefore seldom killed. Its venom contains a very powerful neurotoxin that acts on the nervous system.

The colour is green, brown or olive with black bands. Length: average 3.5m (11ft) but has been known to grow to 5.5m (17ft).

KRAIT

Deadly poisonous. All kraits produce deadly venom that attacks the nervous system, but they are not aggressive. Kraits are inactive by day. Found in India, Southeast Asia, Malaysia, the Sulawesi and Andaman Islands. It is coloured in black and white or black and yellow bands. Length: 90–150cm (3–5ft).

MALAYAN PIT VIPER

Dangerously poisonous. Found in Southeast Asia and China. It can be grey, red or fawn, with triangular brown markings outlined by lighter scales, and arrow marks on the head. Length: 60–80cm (24–32in).

PUFF ADDER

Dangerously poisonous. Found in African savannas and swamps, and Arabian arid regions. Its colour is a yellowy, light brown or orange with chevron-shaped, dark brown or black bars. Length: average 1.2m (4ft); maximum 1.8m (6ft).

RHINOCEROS VIPER OR RIVER JACK

Dangerously poisonous. Found in equatorial Africa. It has a bright colour with purple to red-brown marks on the back, and is distinguished by scaly horns on its nose. Length: average 75cm (30in).

DOBOIA OR RUSSELL'S VIPER

Deadly poisonous. This snake from Southeast Asia has probably caused more human fatalities than any other species of viper. Found in many areas from India through to Borneo. Its colour is brownish with reddish spots ringed in black in three rows. Length: 1–1.25m (3–4ft).

WAGLER'S PIT VIPER OR TEMPLE VIPER

Dangerously poisonous. Found in Malaysia through to Philippines. Its colour is green with white crossbands edged in blue or purple. Length: average 60cm (2ft).

AUSTRALIAN COPPERHEAD

Dangerously poisonous. A venomous member of the cobra family, dangerous but not aggressive. Found in south Australian and Tasmanian swamps. Its colour is brown, though some are black. Length: average 1.2m (4ft).

105. TRAVELLING THROUGH SNAKE-INFESTED COUNTRY

- Wear strong leather boots; most snake fangs cannot penetrate tough boot leather.
- Watch where you step; snakes are often sluggish and can easily be stepped on.
- Do not turn stones over with your hands; use a stick.
- Keep looking above your head, some snakes live in trees.
- Do not corner, pick up or provoke a snake.

Should you encounter a snake, stay calm and back away slowly. Chances are, the snake is more surprised than you and will want to make its escape.

If you must kill a snake, hit it hard on the back of the head with a long stick. Make certain that the snake is well and truly dead, as a wounded snake can be ferocious.

Regularly check clothes and rucksacks before putting them on. At night shake out your bedding before turning in.

DEALING WITH SNAKE BITES

Snakes are probably the most instinctively feared of the world's land creatures, and in many cases, quite rightly so. Apart from Europe, which has to contend only with the adder, most other continents have poisonous and lethal species of snake. Snake venom acts differently according to the type of snake. In some cases, the only injury will be localized swelling and torn skin. However, in many cases, there are systemic implications, which will produce results ranging from respiratory arrest to an attack on the central nervous system of the body.

BITE MARKS

If a person has been bitten by a snake, look at the bite marks: these can sometimes inform you whether the snake was poisonous or not. One or two larger puncture wounds at the front of the bite, distinct from the rest, suggest that it was poisonous. Do not, however, assume that all bites from poisonous snakes mean that venom has actually been injected. When snakes bite out of fear rather than for food, they may not actually inject. You will know if they have injected any venom: there will be immediate swelling at the wound site, and the casualty's overall condition will deteriorate. However, you should be careful that the last is not due simply to an hysterical reaction.

Once the casualty has been bitten, regardless of whether symptoms have appeared or not, your main priority above all is evacuation. Try to note the type of snake. If you are unable to identify it, at least note down distinguishing features for the doctors. There is little you can do to negate the effect of the venom itself (unless you have been specifically supplied with antivenins, and that is unlikely). Your priority is basic life support and slowing the circulation of the poison around the system.

Try to calm the victim as much as possible to slow their heartbeat. Wash the wound site with soap and water to remove any poison that might remain. Then tie a restricting bandage (never a tourniquet) around the bitten limb above the bite site; if the casualty has been bitten on the hand, tie the bandage just above his elbow. This should be tight, but ensure that it is not so tight that it restricts blood flow. You can check this by pinching the finger- or toe-nails. The effect of the bandage is to restrict the infusion of the venom through the lymphatic system. However, if you find it difficult to control the pressure and are cutting off the victim's circulation, untie the bandage immediately.

In addition to biting snakes, there are also spitting snakes, which spray venom over some distances, often directed at the eyes. The effect can be excruciatingly painful, and you should immediately wash out the eyes with water. In an absolute emergency and if there is no water close to hand, you can use urine instead.

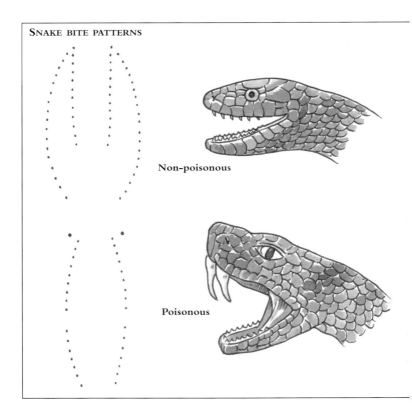

SNAKE BITE PATTERNS

Non-poisonous

Poisonous

One final point on snakebites: never try to suck out the poison. This will only endanger you and the casualty even more.

Aspirin can help to reduce the pain, but the casualty should be evacuated if they become ill from the bite or if the swelling is severe. Time is of the essence – in this situation, you must move quickly.

106. DANGEROUS OR UNPLEASANT INSECTS AND SPIDERS

Though the main dangers in jungle areas are from snakes and large wild animals, there is a great number of insects that inflict a bite or poisonous sting. They may also transmit diseases. The following creepy crawlies are the ones to avoid:

ANTS
Red ants nest in the twigs of trees and shrubs and will bite persistently. African termites build nests with overlapping, mushroom-shaped layers (on rotting trees, for example).

BLACK WIDOW OR HOURGLASS SPIDER
Dangerously poisonous. Named because of its antisocial habit of devouring the male after mating. Males are only half the size of the female and are rarely seen and harmless.

The female's bite is poisonous to humans. It produces local pain and swelling, nausea and difficulty in breathing, and is sometimes fatal. Found in warm areas worldwide. Small and dark with hourglass markings on the abdomen.

CENTIPEDES
Found worldwide in damp areas. Mostly harmless, but some larger varieties can cause swellings and infections.

HORNETS, BEES AND WASPS
These can be found in a variety of forms worldwide. They are best left undisturbed. Stings from several hornets can kill. Wasps tend to attack moving targets, but if a swarm is attacking, run through dense undergrowth.

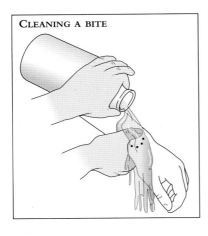

CLEANING A BITE

LEECHES

Leech is the common name for carnivorous or bloodsucking worms. Heat, petrol or alcohol should make them drop off. You can also try applying nicotine or raw lime. Carry out regular checks for leeches and brush off those that have not yet got a hold.

MOSQUITO

Mosquitoes, as many people will know, are deadly. The anopheles mosquito carries malaria, and malaria pills provide less than 50 per cent protection against its bite. Always use a mosquito net, if available. If not, improvise with cloth, parachute or large leaves. Particularly at night, tuck trouser legs into socks and shirt sleeves into gloves. Keep a fire smoking at night, and keep away from swampy or areas containing stagnant pools of water, which is where mosquitoes breed.

SCORPIONS

Dangerously poisonous. They can be found in tropical jungles and are usually darker than the desert varieties. In most species, the sting is painful, but not fatal to humans. However, the sting of one species found in the United States has proved fatal to young children and is potentially fatal to adults. Some jungle varieties can be up to 20cm (8in) long.

TARANTULA

Poisonous, but the bite is not dangerous. Whenever filmmakers need to frighten their audiences, they always use tarantulas. They are large and hairy and have gained a sinister reputation. The poison is not as dangerous as their appearance suggests, but it will cause skin irritation.

TICKS

Ticks breed in grassy areas and are blood-sucking parasites that can spread infectious diseases. They are common in the tropics, and like leeches, they should not be pulled off, since they will leave their jaws embedded in your skin. They can be removed in the same way as leeches. If you have caught an animal such as a pig, take care that ticks do not jump off the dead animal on to you.

Keep your boots on to protect your feet against ticks and fleas that can burrow under your toenails or skin to lay their eggs.

- If possible, always camp well away from swampy areas.
- Use insect repellent if you have it. Apply it to all exposed skin and all clothing openings.
- Wear clothing at all times.
- If you have a mosquito net, use it at night.

107. RAFTS – HOW TO BUILD AND USE THEM

In order to get out of trouble, or to reach civilization, you may need to cross water; be it a river or sea crossing, you should know how to do this safely. The dangers should never be underestimated.

All moving bodies of water should be treated with great respect. You are in danger of being swept off your feet by the current or of falling off a raft, of being dangerously affected by the cold or of being caught in some obstacle like a fallen tree.

LOG RAFT

A raft can be constructed from suitable logs – test them to make sure they

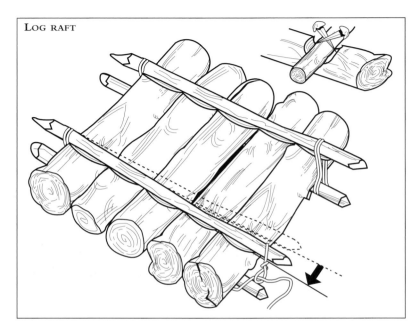

LOG RAFT

float (half in the water and half out). Make sure they are tied to the land when testing and see what their natural flotation properties are – that is, which side will be submerged and which side will form the deck.

When tying the logs together, make sure you cut deep notches into the logs so that the rope or other material you use for binding them does not slip under the twisting action that will take place in the water.

Place the logs over two cross-bars at either end, with the longest log at the centre and logs of the next size down placed on either side symmetrically. This will give you some kind of prow on the raft. Lash the main logs together and then place two bars across the raft at both ends above the other bars. Cut notches in these bars and lash them together to create pressure on the sides. You can add more cross-bars to form a flatter deck, according to how much time you have and how detailed you require the construction to be.

Centre boards, which will act like keels and help to stop the raft drifting sideways, can be pushed down between gaps in the logs and securely lashed. As in all survival matters, you can improvise according to your needs and the available materials.

BAMBOO RAFT

You can cut 3m (10ft) lengths of bamboo (the number will depend on

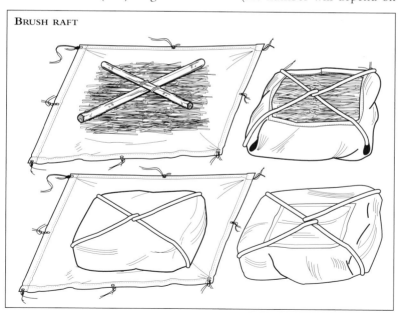

BRUSH RAFT

the number of people using the raft). If you use about 12 lengths, side by side, the raft should be able to take up to four people. In the penultimate bamboo section at each end, cut a hole so that a cross stake can pass through all the lengths of bamboo lying side by side.

Each bamboo cane should then be lashed to the cross stakes. Once you have done this, you can construct a second layer to form a platform, ideally with longer arms on the outside so that the platform can be more easily lashed to the bottom layer. The platform will give the raft depth and improve its flotation.

BRUSH RAFT

Take two ponchos and tie off the necks with the drawstring. Attach ropes to the corners and sides of the ponchos. Spread the poncho on the ground and pile fresh brush onto it to a height of 45cm (18in). Pull the poncho neck drawstring up through the centre of the brush stack. Take two saplings and make an X-frame. Place it on top of the brush stack. Tie it in place with the central poncho neck-drawstrings. Pile another 45cm (18in) of brush on top of this. Pull the poncho sides up around the brush and tie the ropes diagonally across, from corner to corner, and from side to side.

Spread the second poncho, hood up, next to the bundle. Roll the bundle into the centre of the second poncho, tied side-down. Tie the second poncho around the bundle with diagonal ropes and from side to side.

RAFT STEERING

You can construct an A-frame at the back of the raft to hold a steering oar, but the A-frame will need to be firmly constructed and lashed if it is not to collapse. Alternatively, you can use a simpler method, which is to build up the rear of the raft with a couple of logs and then fix the steering oar on top of these in such a way that you will be able to turn it without losing it in the water.

LOG FLOTATION

This simple but effective device can be made quickly with two light logs and some rope or similar material. Place the logs about 60cm (2ft) apart and tie them together, preferably with notches in the logs so that the rope does not slip off. You should then be able to sit between the two logs, with your legs folded over one and your lower back lying against the other. Test the device to make sure your measurements are right and that it works before using it in deeper water. You can improvise other flotation devices, depending on your requirements and the materials available.

108. HOW TO CROSS RIVERS

You will need to choose a suitable spot to cross a river. Look out for:

- A place where you are least in danger of losing your footing, with easy access to the water on one side and a way out on the other side, both of which are safe from any dangerous wildlife. To plan your crossing, you should have a good vantage point; climb a tree if necessary.
- Where the water is shallowest, or where the river is divided up into separate channels that can be negotiated individually, or where there are natural stepping stones.
- Areas to avoid, such as where water is running rapidly over rocks, or where water eddies show that there is an obstacle under water that is creating dangerous back currents. Estuaries, which you also want to avoid, can be wide and prone to awkward tide movements.
- Currents – make allowances for being carried downstream by the current and for missing your ideal landing spot.

WADING ACROSS

- Take your clothes off and store them in a plastic bag in your backpack.
- Keep your boots on to improve traction on the river bed.

- Ensure that your backpack can be easily unhitched from your back if you slip – do not have any buckles holding it on to your body. Hitch it over the downstream shoulder only.
- Take a sturdy pole with you and push it into the river bed upstream in order to help break the current. You can brace yourself against the pole.
- Cross the river at an angle of 45° to the current.

ROPED CROSSING FOR THREE OR MORE PEOPLE

A roped crossing requires a loop of rope measuring about three times as long as the width of the stream. The strongest person should go across first, with the rope tied round his/her chest. The other two let out the rope, making sure it does not snag on any obstacles, ready to haul the first person back if necessary.

When across, number one unties himself/herself and number two ties the rope round their chest. That person's crossing is monitored by rope holders on both banks. Number three then crosses, with one person holding the rope taut on the opposite side, and the other ready to help pull the rope if necessary.

ALTERNATIVE ROPED CROSSING (TYROLEAN)

The strongest person goes ahead and ties the rope to a tree or other firm anchor on the far bank. The rest of the team follow – for example, by hitching a karabiner with a chest harness on to the rope. The back packs can be brought across in a similar way. The last person swims across, with other team members ready to haul him/her in.

SWIMMING

Do not try swimming unless you are confident that you can manage the current (throw bits of wood into the river to test the strength of the current), that it is not too cold and that you will not be tangled up in weed, branches or other obstacles that may be in the river.

You will want to keep your clothes dry, so think of how you can create a waterproof flotation device that you can hold in front of you as you swim, kicking with your legs. Use flotation devices, such as the brush raft described above (see Tip 107), or anything else that will float, to help you cross in safety.

SURVIVING NATURAL DISASTERS

Air travel has opened up the entire world, and we are now travelling to more destinations than ever before. These days, we can easily find ourselves heading for a holiday resort in an area prone to very severe natural storms. It makes sound sense that you be aware both of the potential dangers of the region you are in and of the correct course of action to take. Read as much as you can about the region you are visiting.

The better prepared you are, the easier it will be to cope with whatever nature can throw at you, and the more likely it is you will survive. If you're well prepared, you are also in a better position to help others. It is difficult to think quickly and plan when an emergency is under way and people are panicking. Give yourself an advantage by planning ahead and knowing where your essential equipment is.

Stay informed about meteorological conditions; this may involve carrying a battery-powered radio. Make sure, too, that you have emergency supplies to hand, including:

- Food and water
- First aid kit
- Pocket knife, eating utensils, can opener, etc

- Map
- Torch
- Adequate clothing
- Good shoes or boots

109. EARTHQUAKES

Earthquakes are impossible to predict and can have a number of differen classifications – tectonic, volcanic and artificially produced. No place o earth is free from the danger of an earthquake.

Most earthquakes occur at the edges of tectonic plates. Plates eithe

CITIES IN DANGER OF EARTHQUAKE

Alexandria	Dacca	Lima	Seoul
Algiers	Guatemala	Lisbon	Shanghai
Ankara	City	Los Angeles	Shenyang
Athens	Harbin	Managua	Sian
Bangkok	Havana	Manila	Singapore
Beijing	Hong Kong	Mexico	Surabaya
(Peking)	Istanbul	Milan	Taipei
Bogota	Jakarta	Nanking	Tashkent
Bucharest	Kabul	Naples	Teheran
Cairo	Kanpur	Osaka	Tientsin
Calcutta	Kobe	Pyongyang	Tokyo
Canton	Kuala	Rangoon	Tripoli
Caracas	Lumpur	Rome	Turin
Casablanca	Kunming	San	Wuhan
Chongqing	Lahore	Francisco	Yokohama
Davao	Lanzhou	Santiago	

slide against each other, or one under the other. Earthquakes can also be artificially produced by underground detonation of atomic explosives or the pumping of fluids deep into the earth through wells. For example, in 1962, the city of Denver, Colorado, began to experience earthquakes for the first time in its history when waste fluid was pumped into a deep well at an arsenal to the east of the city. After the pumping was stopped, the tremors continued for a short time, then ceased.

DANGERS

The danger of an earthquake is usually its effect on manmade structures or the triggering of, for example, landslides and tidal waves (tsunamis).

Earthquake effects can be worse on soft ground, particularly mud and clay soils, which tend to amplify the shockwaves. This also applies to water-logged, low-lying regions. Steep slopes can be perilous because of the danger of landslides.

PREPARATION

Put together essential supplies such as water, canned food, a battery-powered radio and a torch. Keep these items at hand at all times.

Try to find out about any local emergency plans.

ACTION

Indoors

If you are inside a building, stay there! Get under a strong table or some other protection and hold on during the tremors. If you cannot get underneath something, get into a doorway or get close to an inside wall. Keep away from heavy objects like book-cases.

Kitchens are dangerous places during earthquakes – get out!

Keep away from any glass, such as windows or mirrors. If you are near windows, cover your face with a coat or something similar.

THE RICHTER SCALE

FORCE OF EARTHQUAKE SCALE	
Not felt but recorded on seismometer	2.6
Widely felt	3.5
Local damage	4.5
Destructive earthquake	6.0
Major earthquake	7.0
Great earthquake	8.0+

Do not run downstairs while the building is shaking.

Do not attempt to run out of a building during an earthquake, as you will be at great risk from falling and flying objects.

Outdoors

Do not try to run away from the earthquake, as you are likely to run into danger. Keep away from trees, buildings or other structures that might fall on you. If you are in the mountains, look out for landslides, avalanches, falling rocks and trees that could be loosened by the quake.

Keep clear of telephone poles, electricity pylons and wires. Never try to touch or move an electric cable that has fallen.

If you are in a car, slow down and drive to a clear place, away from underpasses, lamp-posts or trees. Then stop the car and stay in it until the shaking stops. Once the quake is over, drive slowly and look out for cracks in the road and unevenness caused by earth movement.

SURVIVING THE AFTERMATH OF AN EARTHQUAKE

Take care of one problem at a time:

- Make sure that you are out of any immediate danger. If you get injured, you are no use to yourself or anyone else.
- Find some strong footwear in case you need to climb over debris and broken glass. Be prepared for aftershocks.
- If people are seriously injured, give first aid and make them comfortable, but do not move them unless they are in serious danger of further injury. Seek medical advice for those seriously injured.

THE MERCALLI SCALE

SCALE	FORCE OF EARTHQUAKE
I	Felt by almost no one.
II	Felt by very few people.
III	Tremor noticed, but not recognised as an earthquake.
IV	Felt indoors by many.
V	Felt by almost everyone. Trees and poles swaying.
VI	Felt by everyone. Furniture moved. Slight damage.
VII	Everyone runs outdoors. Considerable damage to poorly built structures.
VIII	Specially designed structures damaged. Others collapse.
IX	All buildings considerably damaged. Cracks in ground.
X	Many structures destroyed. Ground badly cracked.
XI	Almost all structures fall. Bridges wrecked. Wide cracks in the ground.
XII	Total destruction. Waves seen on ground.

- Search your home for any signs of fire and put it out if you can. If the fire is out of control, leave the building immediately.

- If your house uses gas, shut off the main gas valve if you suspect that the pipes have been damaged. Do not use anything that produces a naked flame (for example, matches and camping stoves) until you are certain that there is no gas leak.

- Switch off the electricity at the mains box before attempting any repairs.

- Beware when opening high cupboards, as contents will have shifted and may fall out onto you.

- Check the outside of your building for any damaged chimneys or downed power lines. Do not go near a downed power line or any object that is touching it; let the electricity company deal with it.

FOOD AND WATER

You will probably have no power. Plan to eat first meals made from the contents of your freezer or foods that will spoil, such as vegetables. As long as you open the freezer as little as possible, it should keep food frozen for a couple of days or more.

Do not eat or drink anything that was open during the earthquake, as it will have a high chance of being contaminated with fragments of glass.

Your water supply may also be broken, so take stock of how much water you have in the water heaters, canned food (especially vegetables), and in ice cubes.

STAY CALM!

Remember that the emergency services have prepared disaster plans that do not include answering the telephone! In fact, avoid using the telephone, as you could be tying up an emergency line. The emergency services may not be available anyway!

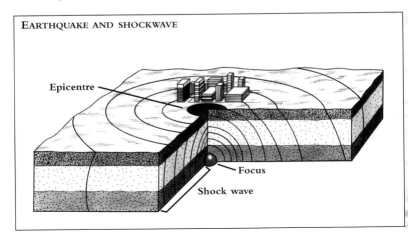

EARTHQUAKE AND SHOCKWAVE

Epicentre

Focus

Shock wave

110. HURRICANES

A hurricane is a storm with winds of between 120 and 320km/h (75 and 199mph). Hurricanes have their source in equatorial waters, particularly the Caribbean Sea and the Gulf of Mexico. In the western Pacific Ocean, they are known as typhoons; in the Indian Ocean and around Australia, they are known as tropical cyclones.

DANGERS

The destructive power of a hurricane can be manifested in different ways, including wind power, rainfall and storm surges.

The storm surge is the most dangerous aspect of the hurricane, accounting for 90 per cent of deaths. It is caused by changes in atmospheric pressure inside the hurricane sucking up the sea. Hurricane winds also pile up the water against the coastlines. The resulting wall of water can be up to 12m (40ft) high, though it diminishes as it heads inland.

FORECAST

It is difficult to forecast a hurricane. Even meteorological offices in developed countries can be caught with their guard down, with devastating consequences.

Hurricanes tend to be more prolific in the Atlantic region in August and September. The source of the hurricane consists of warm water influenced by the earth's rotation. The sea temperature must be at least 26°C (79°F) for a hurricane to form.

Hurricanes occur at least 4–5° polewards from the equator, and certainly no closer.

When there is a threat of a hurricane occurring within the next 24–36 hours, a Hurricane Watch is issued. If a hurricane is expected in less than 24 hours, a Hurricane Warning is issued. During a hurricane watch, listen to a battery powered radio for updates and make preparations.

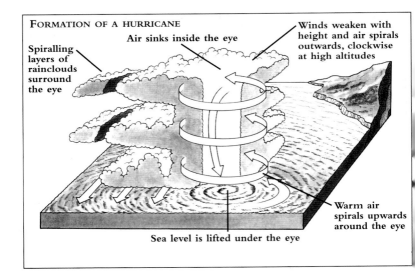

FORMATION OF A HURRICANE

Air sinks inside the eye

Winds weaken with height and air spirals outwards, clockwise at high altitudes

Spiralling layers of rainclouds surround the eye

Warm air spirals upwards around the eye

Sea level is lifted under the eye

PREPARATION

Start by boarding up windows; just taping up windows will not help. Trim any weak branches off trees that may be near houses. Bring inside any objects, such as garbage cans or garden chairs, that could be picked up by the wind.

ACTION

Inside

Shelter in the cellar, or somewhere away from windows or the roof. A hurricane can rip off the roof. Do not drop your guard when the calm eye of the storm passes over. The other side of the storm, with winds travelling in the opposite direction, will soon reach you.

SAFFIR-SIMPSON SCALE OF STORM INTENSITY		
STORM	CATEGORY	WIND SPEED (MPH)
Tropical storm		31–73
Hurricane	Level 1 (Weak)	74–95
	Level 2 (Moderate)	96–110
	Level 3 (Strong)	111–130
	Level 4 (Very strong)	131–155
	Level 5 (Devastating)	156–

Outside

Find a cave, ditch or rocky outcrop to shelter in or under. Be prepared to adjust your position when the eye of the storm has passed over.

Do not attempt to drive anywhere in a car in a hurricane. Take care with bridges, which may be washed away.

111. TORNADOES

Hurricanes can spawn tornadoes, which are much more unpredictable. The track of a tornado is erratic, and so all the more dangerous. A tornado will not give you time to plan and think. Be ready to act fast.

The name comes from the Latin *tonare*, to thunder. A tornado looks like a grey spiral, funnel or elephant's trunk, and wind speeds can be anything from 480 to 560km/h (298 to 348mph).

Generally, tornados rotate anticlockwise in the northern hemisphere and clockwise in the southern, but the occasional tornado reverses this behaviour.

It is made visible by the dust that is sucked up by the winds and by condensed water droplets. The area of the tornado touching the ground is usually only a few hundred metres (several hundred feet) across, though it can be up to 1km (⅔ mile) wide. A tornado can cause a house to tear apart by creating higher pressure inside the house than outside.

When a tornado develops out at sea, it is generally weaker and these types are usually called waterspouts.

PREPARATION

Find a cellar or tornado shelter in good time before the storm arrives. Remember that, even if the tornado does not appear to be heading in your direction, it may suddenly change course.

ACTION

Inside

Head for shelter in the basement or lowest floor of the building. Stay in

FUJITA-PEARSON TORNADO SCALE

FORCE	SPEED	EFFECT
F–0	64–115km/h (40–72mph)	Chimney damage, tree branches broken
F–1	116–179km/h (73–112mph)	Mobile homes overturned
F–2	180–251km/h (113–157mph)	Considerable damage, mobile homes demolished, trees uprooted
F–3	252–328km/h (158–205mph)	Roofs and walls torn down, trains overturned, cars thrown
F–4	329–416km/h (206–260mph)	Well-constructed walls levelled
F–5	417–509km/h (261–318mph)	Houses lifted off foundations and carried considerable distances; cars thrown as far as 100m (330ft)

the centre of the room, away from corners and windows. Shelter under strong furniture, such as a heavy table, and hold on. Protect your head and neck with your folded arms.

Outside

Do not walk around outside – you could be plucked up by the wind or be struck by heavy objects thrown by the wind.

Do not stay in a car, but get out and find the most solid shelter available, or shelter in a ditch if necessary or under a rocky outcrop. Tornados often suck up cars and throw them around like toys.

112. HOW TO AVOID BEING STRUCK BY LIGHTNING

Lightning is a visible electrical discharge between clouds, or between a cloud and the earth. More people in the developed world are killed by lightning than by any other natural phenomenon except floods. It is, however, easier to protect yourself from lightning than from an earthquake or a hurricane or tornado.

FORMATION OF A TORNADO

When thunderstorms are in your area but not directly overhead, the threat of lightning is still real even if it is sunny with clear skies and not raining.

PREDICTION

Although there is such a thing as a bolt from the blue (lightning out of a clear, blue sky), the most likely source of lightning is dark thunderclouds. If you see them approaching, take precautions.

Lightning is accompanied by thunder. Since light travels faster than sound, you can estimate the distance in miles between yourself and a thunderstorm by counting the seconds that elapse between the lightning and the thunder, and dividing by five. You are still in danger from lightning, even if the storm is far away.

PROTECTION

You can protect a building from lightning by attaching a metallic rod, wired to the ground, to the highest part of the roof. Lightning is attracted to metal objects and that way, if the house is struck, the force of the lightning bolt will be channelled harmlessly into the ground.

ACTION

Inside

Stay away from telephones, electrical appliances, computers and, in particular, televisions. Do not use taps in sinks or bathtubs because metal pipes and water conduct electricity.

Outside

Do not shelter under a single tree, as the lightning is likely to strike the tree. Lie flat on the ground if you are exposed in a thunderstorm. Find a ditch or depression to lie in.

Should you start to feel your hair standing on end out in the open, bend forward and put your hands on your knees. Adopt a low crouching position with your feet together and hands on ears to minimize thunder shock. Remove any metal objects.

If you need to take shelter in a cave, make sure you go deep inside if possible. Do not stay near the mouth of the cave.

- Avoid water.
- Avoid high ground.
- Avoid open spaces.

TREATING PEOPLE WHO HAVE BEEN STRUCK BY LIGHTNING

If treated immediately, people can survive a lightning strike. If several people have been struck at the same time, call the emergency services and then treat the 'apparently dead' first. The ones who are unconscious but still breathing will probably recover on their own.

Move victims to a safer location. People struck by lightning do not carry a charge, so do not be afraid to touch them.

If the person is not breathing, start mouth-to-mouth resuscitation. Check their pulse at the carotid artery (side of the neck) and if no pulse is present start CPR (cardio-pulmonary resuscitation) immediately.

If the casualty's pulse returns, continue ventilation for as long as needed. If no pulse returns after about 30 minutes of continuous CPR, stop resuscitation.

113. FLOODS

Floods are a common and very dangerous form of natural disaster, especially for the large part of the earth's population that live beside coasts, river deltas and estuaries.

After rainfall, water is absorbed by the soil and vegetation, or by evaporation. The remainder, called the runoff, runs into streams and rivers.

The heavier the rainfall, the greater the runoff. When the runoff is too large, and streams and rivers cannot contain it, a flood is caused. Intense rainfall over a small area causes flash floods.

PREPARATION

Find out about the water level at flood stage in the place you are staying. Fill bathtubs, sinks and buckets with clean water, in case the water supply becomes contaminated. Keep in touch with flood warnings on a battery operated radio.

ACTION
Inside

Collect vital supplies and move to an upper part of the house. Be prepared, if necessary, to climb out on to the roof.

Take warm clothing. Take some rope with you to tie yourself and others to a stable structure like a chimney stack if you are on the roof.

Outside

Make your way to high ground. Do not, if at all possible, wade through flood water. If absolutely necessary, perform the routine for river crossings as described in Tip 108.

If you are in a vehicle that has stalled, abandon it and get to high ground as quickly as possible.

114. TSUNAMI

Tsunami is a Japanese word meaning 'harbour wave'. It is caused by earthquakes with vertical movement that creates water displacement. It is often mistakenly called a tidal wave, but is not caused by the gravitational forces involved in tides.

The wavelength of a tsunami can be up to 200km (124miles) and travel for hundreds of kilometres across deep ocean, reaching speeds of up to 800km/h (497mph). When the wave enters shallow coastal waters, the wave, which may have been only 50cm (20in) high out at sea, suddenly grows rapidly. When the wave hits the shore, it can be 15m (45ft) or more high.

Tsunamis have a tremendous energy that moves an enormous volume of water capable of destroying coastal towns. A tsunami should not be confused with storm surges, which are domes of water that rise underneath hurricanes or cyclones and cause massive coastal flooding when they hit land. In 1970, an estimated 500,000 people were killed in Bangladesh by a storm surge that followed a cyclone.

Most tsunamis originate along the so-called 'ring of fire', a zone of volcanoes and seismic activity 32,500km (20,195 miles) long that encircles the Pacific Ocean. Forty tsunamis have hit the Hawaiian Islands since 1819.

PREDICTION

It is difficult to predict a tsunami from the behaviour of waves at sea, since tsunami waves might travel a long way at a height of no more than 1m (3ft) and therefore pass by ships unnoticed. But, by the time they reach land they have gained in height significantly,. Japan's worst tsunami involved a wave 24m (80ft) high.

Tsunami alerts are issued on the basis of earthquake reports. Although this system can work well for places that are far enough away from the earthquake, it is often the case that the tsunami will have struck before the warning can be given.

Keep in touch with earthquake warnings, and beware of any unusual rumblings.

PREPARATION

Plan an escape route to an inland location that is above the likely height of any approaching wave. Put together an emergency kit with food and first aid equipment.

ACTION

Do not head towards the beach to check if you can see a wave approaching. If you can see it, it is too late to escape. Remember that a series of waves may be involved, so do not return to the danger area until there is a complete all-clear.

115. DROUGHTS

In the United States drought is defined as less than 2.5mm ($\frac{1}{10}$in) of rainfall in 48 hours. In Britain, an absolute drought is defined as a period of 15 days with less than 0.25mm ($\frac{1}{100}$in) of rain each day. In India, a drought is declared if the rainfall is less than 75 per cent of the average.

Major droughts tend to occur at latitudes of about 15–20°, in areas that border on the permanently dry areas of the world. Due to unpredictable rainfall, Africa is more at the mercy of droughts than any other area. Seasonal rainfall in Africa can show large variations within the season itself, and tends to fall in short and intense storms. The rain can also be very localized.

PREPARATION

You will need to have a store of water and take care that water supplies do not become contaminated during a drought. Ensure that all water is boiled before drinking.

(See Tips 49–52 for advice on finding water in arid regions.)

FIRE

Aridity and drought can lead to bush fires. Australia is especially prone to these, with the native eucalyptus tree being a prime culprit in the spread

TYPES OF DROUGHT

METEOROLOGICAL DROUGHT	An unusual precipitation for a particular region during a certain time scale. A continued period without rainfall.
AGRICULTURAL DROUGHT	Inadequate soil moisture for the growth of particular plants in certain regions.
HYDROLOGICAL DROUGHT	Reduced precipitation for an extended period; usual water supplies, such as lakes, rivers and reservoirs, are deficient.
SOCIOECONOMIC DROUGHT	Water supplies are so low that the community is adversely affected.

of fire. There tends to be a great deal of dry bark and other matter on the floor of Australian forests, providing good fuel for fires. The amount of litter and the time that has elapsed since the last fire are critical in judging how intensely a fire will burn.

PREVENTION

Take great care when lighting a camp fire, especially in a dry area. Use a constructed fireplace or light the fire in a trench at least 30cm (12in) deep.

Take care that tree roots do not catch fire. Clear the ground in the area at least 3m (10ft) from the campfire. Do not light a fire when conditions are hot and windy, and when the bush is very dry.

If you see a fire starting, use a branch with green leaves to damp it down or use any available fire-fighting equipment, such as poles with flaps on the end that can be found in most forests. Do not swing the flames around and thus spread the fire. Remember that fires burn more rapidly uphill and that burnt material can roll down the hill.

TYPES OF FIRE

GROUND FIRE	Burns below the surface of the earth in layers of organic material such as peat. They tend to smoulder, have no flame and little smoke. They are difficult to control.
SURFACE FIRE	Includes grass fires and forest fires that burn debris on the forest floor. They can also burn the lower branches of trees.
CROWN FIRE	Burns the tops of trees, and they are dangerously unpredictable. They can burn ahead of the surface fire.
SPOT FIRE	Caused by burning leaves and bark being blown ahead of the main fire, and causing secondary fires elsewhere, sometimes many kilometres away.

ACTION

If you are trapped by a fire, try to crouch in a pond, lake or river, or look for shelter in a clear area or among rocks. Lie flat and cover your body and head with wet clothing or with soil. Breathe the air close to the ground to avoid scorching your lungs or inhaling smoke.

As a last resort, if you see an opening, and the fire is not too deep or too high, you can attempt to dash through the flames to the area behind them that has already been burnt. You will need to be absolutely resolved to go all the way through and not try to turn back, so be sure. If the flames are higher than head height, do not attempt to run through them.

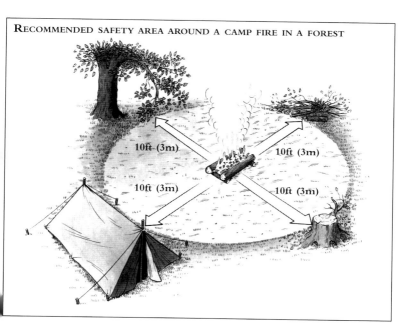

RECOMMENDED SAFETY AREA AROUND A CAMP FIRE IN A FOREST

10ft (3m) 10ft (3m)

10ft (3m) 10ft (3m)

If you decide to dash through the flames, cover as much of the surface of your body as possible and dampen clothes and hair if you have water. If your clothes catch light, do not stay on your feet once out of the fire, but crouch down.

Do not try to escape a fire by running uphill, unless absolutely necessary since fire burns more rapidly uphill.

116. VOLCANIC ERUPTIONS

Volcanoes are formed by the outpouring of lava and by other fragment material. There are a number of active volcanoes around the world and some volcanoes are dormant. Mount Vesuvius near Naples and Etna in Italy represent two of the active volcanoes in Europe.

DANGERS

When a volcano erupts, lava mixed with steam and other gases is forced out of the earth and forms an impenetrable cloud. The lava rises inside the vent of the volcano, some pieces shoot up into the air and some flows over the crater. More lava may emerge from a secondary vent in the side of the volcano.

The lava flow is generally slow-moving, though this is not always the case. Pahoehoe is a smooth lava that forms a ropey surface. Aa is sharp and twisted, much like clinker, and tends to flow faster than pahoehoe. The latter flows at about 1m (3ft) per minute, though if the slope is steep and the lava emission is heavy, this speed can increase to 400m (1200ft) per minute, which can overtake a person attempting to flee it. Aa tends to move in surges, piling up each time before moving on.

As well as lava, the volcano can throw out material, which ranges from fine ash to 8-tonne bombs that can travel up to 5km (3 miles). This flying material, or pyroclastic flow, is the most dangerous element of any volcano, since the lava itself, with a certain amount of warning, can be avoided without too much difficulty.

Another highly destructive characteristic of some volcanoes is *nuée ardente*, or glowing clouds. These are ground-hugging clouds of molten lava fragments that can move with great speed down a mountain.

SECONDARY EFFECTS

Secondary effects from a volcano include earthquakes (normally preceding the eruption), flash floods, landslides and mudflows, thunderstorms and tsunamis.

In Colombia, in 1985, a volcano precipitated a landslide of mud and rock, which buried a whole town and its inhabitants. Since the soil on the edges of volcanoes is fertile, larger numbers of people than ever before are willing to take the risk of living in the danger area. The presence of other people does not mean it is safe.

PREDICTION

It is difficult to predict accurately a volcanic eruption, just as it is difficult to predict an earthquake. One of the best indications of timing is the record of the particular volcano, which will give a fair idea of when it is likely to erupt again. An earthquake almost invariably precedes an eruption, though the timescale can vary from hours to months.

PREPARATION

Be aware of the warning systems in your area. Remember that some countries have better warning systems than others, so be prepared to make your own judgements about danger signs when necessary. Always err on the side of caution, since even highly experienced volcanologists have been killed by volcanoes.

Make sure you have an evacuation plan prepared. Ideally, this should involve getting to high ground as far away from the eruption as possible. Also prepare an alternative route.

ACTION

Equip yourself with goggles and some kind of breathing mask. If you do not have a mask, hold a damp cloth over your face to help you breathe. Avoid low-lying areas if possible, as you will be in danger from flash floods.

Do not cross a low-lying area or go over a bridge if there is a mud-flow approaching. Remember, you cannot outrun a mud-flow!

SURVIVING THE AFTERMATH OF A VOLCANIC ERUPTION

As a survivor, you are still faced with major problems in the days follow-

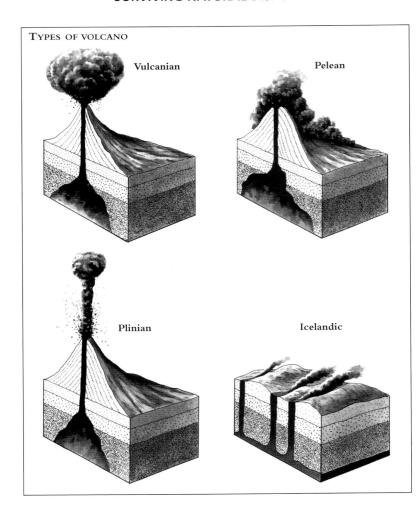

TYPES OF VOLCANO

Vulcanian

Pelean

Plinian

Icelandic

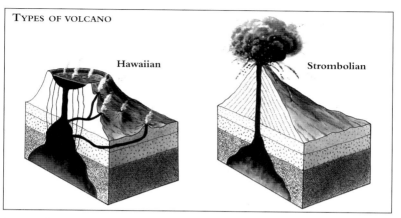

TYPES OF VOLCANO

Hawaiian

Strombolian

ing a volcanic eruption. Beware of inhaling ash – keep a mask on or use a damp cloth. Keep goggles on.

Beware of the danger of heavy ash, which can collapse roofs, and be aware of the dangers posed by landslides and mud-flows.

LANDSLIDE AND MUD-FLOW

There is usually little or no warning of a landslide or mud-flow, but the following signs can be an indication:

Inside

Doors stick; cracks appear in plaster, tiles and bricks. Shelter under a sturdy object, such as a table, and hold on.

Outside

Cracks begin to appear in the ground and pavement; water comes out of the ground in places that it normally doesn't; fences and trees move; there is a rumbling sound.

Get out of the path of the landslide or mud-flow – remember, you cannot outrun it. Head for the nearest high ground, which is out of the direct path of danger. If you are caught, curl up in a ball and protect your head.

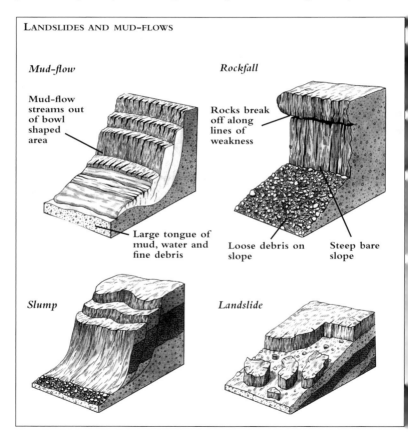

LANDSLIDES AND MUD-FLOWS

Mud-flow

Mud-flow streams out of bowl shaped area

Large tongue of mud, water and fine debris

Rockfall

Rocks break off along lines of weakness

Loose debris on slope

Steep bare slope

Slump

Landslide

BEWARE

There may be a multitude of accidents waiting to happen after any of the above emergencies have occurred. Watch out for:

- Fallen power lines, which could electrocute you if you touch them. There may be damage to electrical systems within buildings.
- Ruptured gas mains and burst sewage pipes. Ruptured water pipes will mean that you may have contaminated water. Dangerous flammable or toxic fluids and materials are some of the many other dangers you will have to face.
- Aftershocks that can bring down weakened structures.
- Animals, even tame ones, may become more dangerous. Treat all animals with caution.

Use your common sense, and proceed with caution.

Finally, do not forget to help others in need, such as children, anyone who has been injured and the elderly.

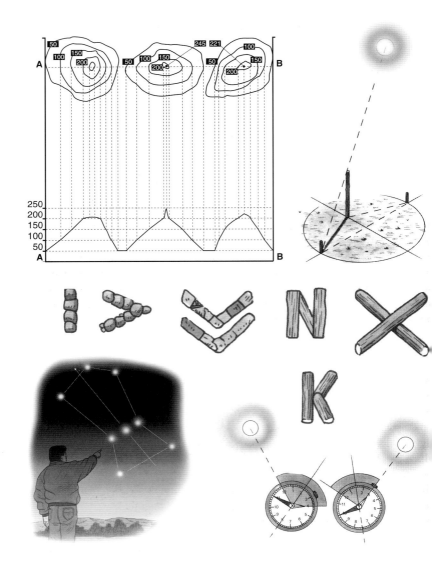

NAVIGATION AND SIGNALLING

Move from your shelter only when it becomes obvious that no-one is searching for you, or your present position presents serious objective dangers. To reach your way to safety, being able to use a map and compass, or other means, and/or being able to signal correctly to potential rescuers is a simple set of skills that anyone can learn and which may save your life. Indeed, you should make yourself familiar with map reading and navigation techniques before setting out on a major expedition.

117. UNDERSTANDING MAPS

A map uses lines and symbols to portray a certain geographic area, along with its fixed features that can range from mountains and cuttings to footpaths and bars.

Ordnance Survey maps typically have a set of symbols that can be easily understood and which are also explained on the side of the map. Not all maps explain their symbols, so before setting out on a journey into a potentially hazardous environment, make sure that you are familiar with the symbols on the map you are using. It is far better to take with you a reliable and familiar map, such as an Ordnance Survey one, than expect to pick up a map you will be able to understand in the area you are visiting.

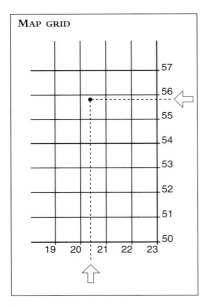

SCALES

The scale of a map will be represented in either words or figures, such as 1:50,000 – this means that one unit of measurement on the map represents 50,000 of the same unit on the ground. For example, on a scale of 1:25000, 1mm on the map = 25m (82ft) on the ground.

MEASURING STRAIGHT-LINE DISTANCE

The measurement to the right of zero on the map scale is called the primary scale. The measurement to the left of zero is called the secondary scale. The secondary scale has the primary unit of measurement – for example, a kilometre divided into blocks, typically of 10m (33ft). If you want to measure the distance between two points on the map, mark the points on the edge of a piece of paper. Place the right mark on a point in the primary scale with the left point falling on the secondary scale to measure whatever fraction of a kilometre or mile you wish to ascertain.

If you want to measure the distance along a road or track, it is best to use a piece of paper. Place one end at the start and follow the road with the edge of the paper until the road turns away from the paper. Mark the point and swivel the paper round on the pencil until it reaches the road again, and so on.

118. PLOTTING A POSITION

This provides a straightforward and accurate means of finding a position on a map, and it is governed by easily understood rules. The vertical lines on a map are called Eastings and the horizontal lines are called Northings. You always read the Eastings first and the Northings second.

SIX-FIGURE GRID REFERENCE

You read the first half of a printed grid reference along the horizontal grid line, representing Eastings. The last figure of that half will represent tenths of the grid square, letting you estimate the appropriate distance across the grid square (for example, a figure of 5 means the location is halfway across the grid square). Then follow the same procedure for the second half of the grid reference along the vertical grid line. See the example opposite of 204559.

119. UNDERSTANDING CONTOURS

A contour is usually a brown/ orange line on a map that joins areas of the same height. It is a useful way of gauging the lie of the land. There are other ways of showing elevation, such as hachures (short parallel lines), hill shading and layer tints, but these are not as accurate as contours. In addition to contour lines, the map reader can use spot heights and trig points (see below), and conventional signs to judge elevation.

Contour lines on a map are always the same distance apart – 10m (33ft), for example. The spacing of contour lines indicates the nature of the slope. Evenly spaced and wide apart lines (A): a gentle, uniform slope; evenly spaced and close together (B): a uniform, steep slope; and a ticked contour (C): a vertical or near vertical slope. (See the diagram overleaf).

Other points to note about contours are:

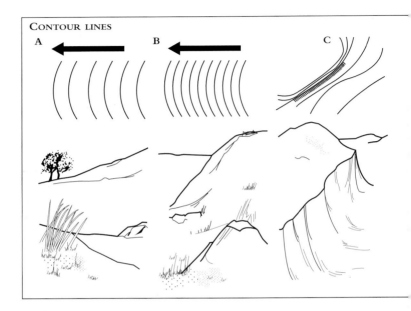

- They always form a v-shape when they cross a river.
- They will not show every regularity of the ground that is below the height of the vertical interval between the contours – in other words they will not record a change in height of 5m (16ft) if the contour spacing is 10m (33ft).
- A road or path along which a contour runs is likely to be level.
- A stream is always in a valley and a lake or pond in a depression.

SPOT HEIGHT

Normally a black point on the map with a figure beside it showing the exact height above sea level at that point. It is not represented on the ground.

TRIG POINT

A small triangle on the map with a dot in the centre shows the altitude as well as the location used in survey triangulations. Trig points are represented on the ground by small triangular concrete blocks, which can be seen as the tops of many major hills.

DRAWING A CROSS-SECTION OF THE GROUND BETWEEN TWO POINTS

Draw on your map a line of the ground you want to see in cross-section. (See page 240). Draw a second line, of the same length, horizontally on a piece of paper to represent ground level (A–B). Then, above and parallel to this ground level, draw lines to mark the contour heights – for example, 50, 100, 150, and so on. Mark every point on the map where the line crosses a contour, and transfer this data to your duplicate line on the paper. Raise a perpendicular line from each point to mark the appropriate height. Join up all these points to reveal a cross-section of the ground.

120. USING A SILVA COMPASS

Using a Silva compass, you can point the arrow on the front of the compass in the direction you wish to go. Then turn the dial so that the north mark is in line with the red compass needle. Your bearing will be shown by the black marker, in line with the direction-of-travel arrow. It is relatively easy to stay on the correct bearing by keeping the marker of north on the compass lined up with the compass needle.

To work out your course from a map, place the side of your compass on a line between your position and your objective. Turn the compass dial until the marked orientating lines on the dial are parallel with the north–south lines on the map, with the orientating arrow pointing north. Note the reading on the marker line and then add the required number of mils for magnetic variation. The compass is now set on the correct bearing.

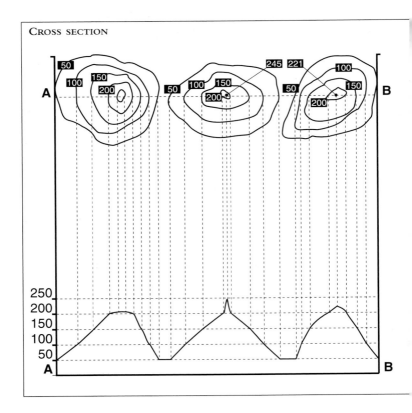

CROSS SECTION

When you take it off the map, you need only turn yourself, with the compass in front of you, until the red needle lies directly on north. You are then facing in the direction you wish to travel.

Once you start out walking on a compass bearing, believe the compass and not your instincts!

121. FINDING YOUR POSITION WITH MAP AND COMPASS

To determine your own position, choose two landmarks that are marked on the map, such as a hill or cairn. Point the arrow on the front of the compass at the first landmark and turn the bowl until the north mark on the compass is lined up with the red compass needle. Note the bearing and subtract the correct number of mils for magnetic variation.

Place the side of the compass on the landmark featured on the map and turn the compass base until the orientating lines in the base of the compass dial are lined up with the north–south grid lines, with the orientating arrow pointing north. Draw a line along the compass base from the landmark.

Repeat the procedure for the second landmark and find your position from where the lines intersect.

122. IMPROVISED COMPASS NEEDLE

You can magnetize a needle by stroking it with a magnet or a piece of silk, repeating the process every few hours to keep it magnetized. Hang the magnetized needle freely from a piece of thread, making sure there are no twists in the thread to influence the needle. The needle should point north.

123. NAVIGATING BY THE SUN

There are a variety of navigation aids, some of which are more reliable than others. It is a good idea to work on the evidence of more than one aid before coming to any firm conclusions.

The sun rises in the east and sets in the west. At midday, the sun is due south in the northern hemisphere, and due north in the southern hemisphere.

USING YOUR WATCH AS A COMPASS

In the northern hemisphere, hold the watch with the hour hand pointing to the sun. Imagine a line travelling through the 12. True south is midway between the hour hand and the 12.

In the southern hemisphere, point the imaginary line through 12 at the sun. True north is the midpoint between the 12 and the hour hand.

TIME AND DIRECTION BY SHADOW

Place the stick at the intersection of the east–west line and the north–south line. Regardless of where you are, the west part of the east–west line shows 0600 hours and the east part 1800 hours. The north–south line becomes the noon line and the shadow of the stick becomes the hour hand.

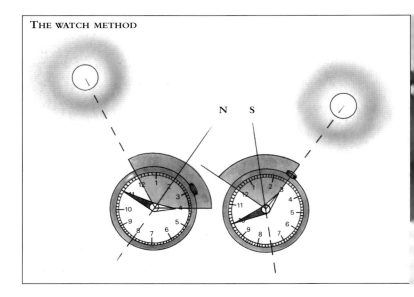

THE WATCH METHOD

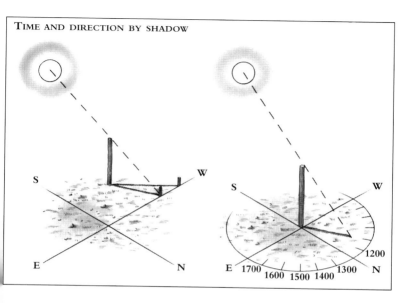

TIME AND DIRECTION BY SHADOW

STICK AND SHADOW

East–west line:

Put a stick about 1m (3ft) high into the ground, which should be flat and clear of debris. Mark the tip of the shadow with a stone. Ten minutes later, mark it again. The straight line between these points marks the east–west line.

North–south line:

Put a stick about 50cm (20in) high into flat ground. With a piece of string, stretched from the stick, draw an arc round the base of the stick, the same radius as the shadow. The shadow will move. When it touches the arc again,

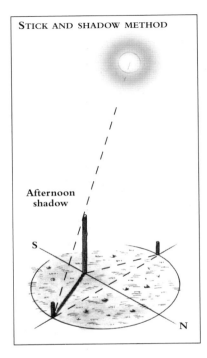

STICK AND SHADOW METHOD

Afternoon shadow

S

N

mark it with a stone or peg. Divide the angle formed by the base of the stick and the two pegs. This will indicate south in the northern hemisphere and north in the southern hemisphere.

124. NAVIGATING BY THE STARS

NORTHERN HEMISPHERE

The North Star or Polaris can be found by following the Plough, Cassiopeia and Orion.

SOUTHERN HEMISPHERE

Multiply the longest axis of the southern cross by 5, which brings you to an imaginary point above the horizon. Your southern landmark will be immediately below the point.

STAR MOVEMENT

Set your eyes on two fixed points on the ground in the distance to help you observe the movements of a star. Look at the star above the points on the ground. If, after a period, the star appears to be rising, you are looking approximately due east. If the star is falling, you are looking approximately due west. If it loops towards the right, you are looking approximately due south, and if it loops towards the left, you are looking approximately due north.

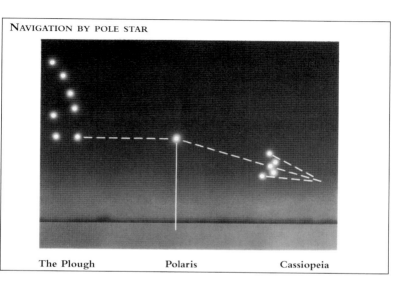

NAVIGATION BY POLE STAR

The Plough   Polaris   Cassiopeia

125. HOW PLANTS INDICATE DIRECTION

You will need practice and experience to draw accurate conclusions about direction from plant growth. Always take as wide a sample as possible and back up the evidence with other means. Certain rules can be followed:

- Flowers tend to grow towards the sun.
- The foliage of trees will be most abundant on the sunny side.
- Moss tends to grow on the damper side of a tree – in other words, the side away from the sun – but this can be influenced by other factors.
- In the northern hemisphere, the rings of a tree stump will be closer together on the south side of the tree, and the bark will also tend to stretch more on the south side.

SOUTHERN CROSS AND ORION

Southern Cross

Orion

126. DEAD RECKONING

This way of estimating distance travelled involves plotting a series of points on your route with the help of a map, compass, protractor, route card and log.

Plot your route on the map, and mark out the distance and direction of each leg of the journey on the route card. When walking, keep a record of the bearing and distance covered in the log. If you have to change direction for any reason, record this in the log.

Work out your average pace, as this will help you to tell how far you have travelled. The average pace is 60–70 double paces per 100m (300ft) on flat, easy ground. You will need to have an idea of the difference in your pace when walking uphill, and also the kind of terrain you are crossing. If you are walking on slippery ground or have shoes with poor traction, you will tend to take shorter paces.

127. SIGNALLING

Signalling will make a great deal of difference to your chances of survival, but you must be able to communicate effectively. You may have only one chance. For example, you do not want to wave frantically at an aircraft only to see the pilot give a friendly wave back and then disappear.

The following tips will teach you a few of the internationally accepted signals that will be instantly recognized by potential rescuers, and also ways to make sure they are likely to be seen. You will need to find the highest and flattest area on which to make your signal.

SIGNALLING EQUIPMENT

Red parachute rocket
Hand flares (pin point red)
Buoyant orange smoke
Sea-dye markers
Signal pistol
Signalling torch
Heliograph (you can use a compact disc)
Personal locator beacon
VHF rescue radio
Whistle
Mirror

128. RADIO PROCEDURE

If you have access to a radio, your chances of rescue are greatly improved. Make sure you know how to use any available radios on an expedition. If you make contact on the radio, it is important that you use the following sequence:

- Mayday, Mayday
- Your call sign (if you have one)
- Your name
- Your location (grid reference)
- Number of survivors
- Grid references of available landing sites
- Inform them if you need special medical help

Listen carefully to instructions from rescuers at all stages. If you are requested to spell out any words, always use the phonetic alphabet. This will help the rescuers and increase the accuracy of the communication.

If you cannot get through using voice, try morse code. Morse code is no longer used as a standard means of radio communication, but when atmospheric conditions are poor, morse can sometimes be heard through the static when voice communication is impossible.

If the radio is equipped with a morse key, all well and good. If not, you will have to improvise. A morse message can be sent by using the clicks of the handset or by using the tuning signal switch.

THE PHONETIC ALPHABET

A Alpha	**B** Bravo	**C** Charlie	**D** Delta
E Echo	**F** Foxtrot	**G** Golf	**H** Hotel
I India	**J** Juliet	**K** Kilo	**L** Lima
M Mike	**N** November	**O** Oscar	**P** Papa
Q Quebec	**R** Romeo	**S** Sierra	**T** Tango
U Uniform	**V** Victor	**W** Whisky	**X** X-Ray
Y Yankee	**Z** Zulu		

MORSE CODE

A .—	M — —	Y —.— —
B —...	N —.	Z — —.. —
C —.—.	O — — —	1 .— — — —
D —..	P .— —.	2 ..— — —
E .	Q — —.—	3 ...— —
F ..—.	R .—.	4 ....—
G — —.	S ...	5 .....
H	T —	6 —....
I ..	U ..—	7 — —...
J .— — —	V ...—	8 — — —..
K —.—	W .— —	9 — — — —.
L .—..	X —..—	0 — — — — —

129. SIGNALLING WITH FLARES

Since you are likely to have a limited supply of pyrotechnics, it is best to use them with care, and only when you consider that they are likely to be seen by a passing aircraft. A red flare indicates distress. A white flare acknowledges or warns.

An aircraft using the Night Search Technique will fire green flares every 5–10 minutes. If you see one or more of these flares:

● Wait for the aircraft to be clear of the glare of its own flares and then fire a red flare, followed by a second flare after a short interval.
● The aircraft will turn towards the first flare if it is seen and check its course on the second one, firing a succession of green lights until it is overhead.
● Wait for the aircraft to be overhead and then fire a third flare. You can also fire the third flare if you think the aircraft is going off course.

Handle flares with great care. Hold them at arm's length and at shoulder height, and make sure they are not pointing at anyone or anything. A hand-held flare has a base cap, which will expose a short string or other safety device. Make sure the flare is pointing up and away before pulling the string or other firing device. Prepare yourself for the recoil from the flare as it ignites. A flare may become hot – make sure you do not drop it on anything that will catch fire, or into the bottom of a lifeboat.

130. SIGNALLING WITH LIGHT AND SOUND

LIGHT

If you are using signal lights, send six flashes in one minute, then allow one minute's pause. Then send six more flashes, and so on. A green light from an aircraft will mean message understood.

SOUND

When using sound, send six signal blasts in one minute, then allow one minute's pause, then six more blasts, and so on. Sound carries further at dusk.

If an aircraft rocks from side to side, it means 'message understood'. If it circles to the right, it means it does not understand the message.

FIRE

Three fires in a triangle is an internationally recognized distress signal. They can also be in a straight line with about a 25m (85ft) gap. It is difficult to maintain three fires over a long period, so if necessary have one burning and two more ready to light if required.

MIRROR

Signals from a mirror or similar reflective material are very effective and can be seen very easily from the air. You can use a suitably burnished shiny object, like the inside lid of your survival tin, or even an old compact disc.

A reflected signal can be seen for up to 100km (62 miles) in normal conditions, and up to 160km (100 miles) in the desert. Don't flash it for too long into the cockpit of a nearby aircraft, as it can blind the pilot. Always practise signalling before you need it – better to get it right first time!

131. MOUNTAIN RESCUE CODE

SOS

Flare signal	Red
Sound signal	3 short blasts, 3 long, 3 short
Light signal	3 short flashes, 3 long, 3 short

HELP NEEDED

Flare signal	Red
Sound signal	6 blasts in quick succession

Light signal   6 flashes in quick succession
Wait one minute, then repeat.

MESSAGE UNDERSTOOD

Flare signal   White
Sound signal   3 flashes in quick succession
Light signal   3 flashes in quick succession

GROUND SIGNALS

Doctor needed

Medical supplies needed

Unable to proceed

Food and water needed

Firearms needed

Map and compass needed

Signal lamp and radio needed

Indicate which direction to follow

Moving in this direction

Will attempt take-off

Aircraft damaged

Safe to land here

Food and oil needed

Everything OK

No

Yes

Not understood

Engineer needed

RETURN TO BASE

Flare signal   Green
Sound signal   Prolonged succession of blasts
Light signal   Prolonged succession of flashes

NATURAL SIGNALS

In snow, you can make a shadow SOS signal by kicking a path in the shape of the letters in the snow. The letters should be about 12m (40ft) high and you can build ridges to emphasize the shadow effect. You can also trace out letters with boughs, or logs.

132. HELICOPTER RESCUE

- To land, a helicopter needs a flat, clear surface with a gradient of no more than 7° (1 in 10) on which to land.
- Clear the site of anything that is likely to be blown up by the downdraught from the helicopter blades, such as loose snow and leaves.
- Mark the landing point with an H made out of flattened rocks or some firmly anchored material. In daylight, use body signals.
- At night, shine torch beams into the sky to attract attention, then down onto the landing point. Do not point them into the pilot's eyes.
- When the helicopter lands, do not approach from the rear, as you can get hit by the rear rotor blades.

133. BODY SIGNALS

These should be made in such a way as to make it obvious to a pilot in an aeroplane or helicopter precisely what you are communicating. If the pilot has understood your message, he will either tilt his wings or flash green signal lights. If he has not understood, he will encircle the aircraft or flash red signal lights.

SURVIVAL FIRST AID

In a survival situation, you may be able to help save somebody's life with only a basic knowledge of First Aid. This can be picked up from books, though finding a centre that can provide practical training is the best option. That way you can be certain that you are learning the correct procedures.

The sequence for administering First Aid should be as follows:

- Is it safe?
- Rapid assessment: ABCDE
- If necessary, institute immediate resuscitation.
- Safe airway position, if appropriate.
- Full assessment: examination techniques.
- Stabilize condition and get help as needed.

IS IT SAFE?

The first thing to ask yourself when you come across a victim is: 'Is it safe?' This means that you should consider whether you will be risking your own life in rushing to the aid of the victim – for example, by running into a busy road.

Once you have checked the potential risks, move the victim to a safe place – for example, dragging them off a road or away from a rockfall. You may need to remove a dangerous object from the vicinity of the victim. Make sure you do not put your own life at risk in the process.

134. ASSESSING A CASUALTY

In survival situations, it is better to have a systematic approach that, when committed to memory, will not fail in times of stress.

The assessment procedure is as simple as A, B, C, D, E:

A - ASSESS

Are there any dangers surrounding the casualty? Look for dangers that may threaten their safety as well as yours. Is it safe to assess the casualty where they are, or will you need to move them? Call or send for help.

B – BREATHING

Is the casualty breathing? Make sure that their airway is clear and open Use the 2-point manoeuvre to lift the chin and tilt the head back. Look listen, feel for breathing. Breathing may be so shallow that you may not be able to detect it easily. Put a mirror to their mouth and check for condensation. If they have stopped breathing, waste no more time assessing them – start artificial respiration immediately.

C – CIRCULATION

Is the heart working? Check the pulse at the carotid (neck) artery. Look feel for major bleeding.

D – DEFORMITY

Ask for information (history). Check body and pockets for identity, medication and constrictions.

Carry out a full head-to-toe examination and compare both sides of the body. Be firm but gentle. Look for bleeding, bruising, pain, loss of function, deformity and swelling.

Place unconscious casualty in the safe airway position.

E – EMOTION

Boost casualty's confidence and hopes by continuing to chat to them. Monitor their vital signs until help arrives.

SAFE AIRWAY POSITION

If there is any danger of spinal injury, particularly to the neck, the spine should be immobilized before moving. If there is no danger of spinal injury, place the victim in the safe airway position, which will stop them choking.

Turn the head of the victim towards you, tilting it back slightly to open the airway. Put the arm that is nearer to you by the side of the victim and slide it under their buttock. Lay the other arm across the victim's chest.

Then place the leg that is further away from you across the one that is nearer to you at the ankle. Pull the victim gently towards you by grasping clothing around the hip with one hand, and support the head with the other hand. Rest the victim against your knees. Bend the top-side leg so that the body does not roll. Keep the head tilted back to maintain an open airway.

EXAMINATION TECHNIQUES

The basic sequence when assessing a victim, unless the symptoms are obvious, is – Look, Feel, Listen.

SAFE AIRWAY POSITION

A general examination should take into account the victim's weight and general fitness, their skin tone and their psychological state.

Lie the patient down and examine the following, from the right of the body – do not miss out anything:

● Hands – check nails and palms for anaemia.
● Pulse – check the rate, rhythm and volume.
● Blood pressure – hypotension is low, hypertension is high.
● Head – eyes, ears, lips and mouth. Feel around the head for swelling and blood.
● Neck – check it is not broken or bruised. Feel down the vertebrae for abnormalities.
● Chest – lungs and heart.
● Abdomen – liver, spleen, kidneys. Ask the casualty if they can feel any pain as you examine them.
● Limbs – look, feel, move. If there are abnormalities ask, talk to the patient as this may be normal for them or a previous injury.

Reassure the patient continuously to boost their confidence and hopes. Continue speaking and maintain body contact even if the patient is unconscious. If the patient is a stranger, introduce yourself.

135. ASSESSING LEVELS OF CONSCIOUSNESS

When attempting to diagnose a casualty's level of consciousness, a degree of subtlety is required on the part of the first-aider, particularly in a survival context. Judging mental state is not just a simple matter of assessing whether or not he or she is conscious, semi-conscious or unconscious, but also means assessing mood swings, temperament, intellectual performance, energy levels and social relations. Such fine levels of assessment are vital in a survival situation. Noticeable alterations in mental state may be due to personality, but they can also signal the early stages of serious environmental illnesses, such as hypothermia, heatstroke, exhaustion, dehydration, impending convulsion, or altitude sickness. If you notice a change in personality in one of your companions, ask yourself the following questions:

- Has the person been exposed to a particular climatic condition for an extended period?
- Is the change in mental state truly uncharacteristic of his or her behaviour? Does he or she appear over-emotional or aggressive?
- Does the person appear to be confused and less responsive? Is their physical movement uncoordinated or clumsy?
- Has the person recently complained of, or sustained, any injuries or illnesses?

USE THE AVPU SCALE

Beyond changes of personality, there are deteriorations in consciousness that can lead eventually to full unconsciousness, a condition that should always be taken very seriously. Unconsciousness occurs when the normal patterns of brain activity are interrupted and can result in minor disorders, such as a fainting fit, or major brain damage or respiratory/circulatory failure.

A = Alert
The casualty is fully conscious, aware of his position, and is able to interact fully with the outside world.

V = Voice
At this level of consciousness, the casualty is still responding to your voice, though they may be sluggish or incoherent. To test this level of response, give the person simple commands to follow, such as getting them to blink their eyes or squeeze your hand if they can hear you.

- **P = Pain**

  The casualty seems to respond only to pain. Try inducing particularly sensitive pains or sensations, such as squeezing the ear lobe or scratching the soles of the feet. If the person tries to pull away or moves, there is still activity being processed between the nerves, spinal cord and brain.

- **U = Unresponsive**

  This is a very serious state – the casualty is totally unconscious and does not react to any form of stimulus.

Using this scale enables you to make a judgement as to the seriousness of the casualty's condition, but you should make regular checks of the casualty's vital signs. A casualty may become unconscious due to problems with circulation, breathing and hydration. If the casualty is fully unconscious, they are prone to asphyxiation through airway obstruction (by vomit or tongue). As you start to deliver treatment, repeat the AVPU diagnosis continually; this will give you a good indication of whether your treatment is working.

The general rules for dealing with a fully unconscious person are:

- An unconscious person has weakened body systems, so do not move them roughly or make them sit up unless necessary. The person's unconsciousness may be caused by a spinal injury.
- Never give an unconscious person anything whatsoever to eat or drink, as they may choke.
- Keep talking to an unconscious person, as he or she may still be able to hear you, and do not say anything to alarm them.
- Remember that the unconscious casualty has lost his or her usual ability to respond to heat, cold and other climatic phenomena. You will have to protect them from these, especially in very cold environment where hypothermia is a possibility.

● The casualty should never be left alone when unconscious, as his or her condition could change at any moment.

The basic principle to follow with an unconscious casualty is to fully examine them for injuries or illnesses that may be sources of the unconsciousness. These should then be treated in their own right, and consciousness monitored as part of a successful response to treatment.

136. ARTIFICIAL RESPIRATION (MOUTH-TO-MOUTH RESUSCITATION)

If the victim is not breathing, he or she will die in a short time. You must, therefore, restore breathing immediately. (See page 262).

● Clear the airway of any blockages and ensure the victim is on a reasonably firm surface (A).
● Tilt the victim's head backwards and place the heel of your hand on the forehead of the victim so that the chin is raised. With the hand resting on the forehead, pinch the victim's nose with thumb and forefinger (B).
● Take a deep breath, place your mouth tightly over the victim's mouth and blow air from yours into theirs (C).
● Stop blowing when the victim's chest is expanded (D). Lift your hand from the victim and watch for the chest to fall. Give the victim further quick breaths, taking a deep breath yourself between each one.
● Carry on blowing into the victim's lungs at a rate of 12 breaths per minute until the victim begins to breathe on his or her own. You can then stop blowing at this stage.

CARDIO-PULMONARY RESUSCITATION (CPR)

This method is used when the patient has stopped breathing and when there is no pulse. Never perform this technique if there is even a trace of

MOUTH-TO-MOUTH RESUSCITATION

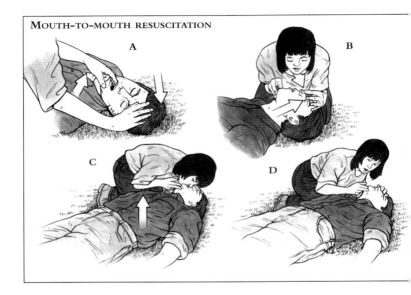

a pulse. It should be performed only by someone who has had training in the method.

- If, after performing artificial respiration, the victim's heart is still not beating, place the heel of one hand on the lower part of the breastbone and place the other hand on top (A).
- Take care when you apply pressure not to damage the ribs (B and D).
- Compress the breastbone 80 times per minute, with a pause every 15 to give the victim two breaths (D).

If there are two people available to help, one should perform the chest compression and the other mouth-to-mouth respiration. This should be a a ratio of one breath per five compressions. You should give 60 compressions per minute with a pause of 1–1½ seconds after every five compressions.

Children and infants

You should exert less pressure and increase the number of compressions per minute. Use two fingers on an infant, compressing 100 times per minute. Take care to depress to only about 2.5cm (1in).

With children up to 10 years, use the heel of one hand and push lightly 90–100 times per minute. Compress by only 3.5cm (1½in). You should give 5 compressions for every lung inflation.

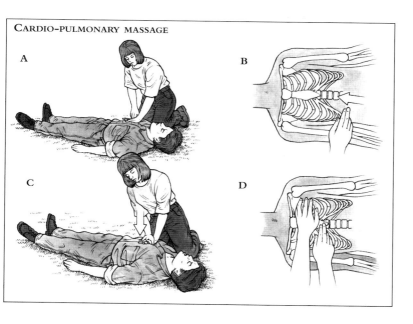

CARDIO-PULMONARY MASSAGE

137. CLEARING A BLOCKED AIRWAY (CHOKING)

Choking is caused by a blockage of the airway, often by food. Signs of choking are a person holding their throat, an inability to cough, a wheezing sound, blue skin (if unconscious), no rise and fall of the chest (if unconscious).

CONSCIOUS VICTIM

Lower the victim's head to below chest level and then administer some blows to the back (A). They should be firm, but take care not to damage the spine. If this does not work, use the 'Heimlich manoeuvre'. Stand behind the victim and place one fist just under the breastbone or sternum (B). Hold the fist with the other hand, and then make a sharp, hard thrusting movement inwards and upwards (C). Note: this is quite a dangerous procedure for a first-aider to carry out: do it only if all other methods have been exhausted, and the casualty is in imminent danger of death.

If you are alone and you are choking, administer abdominal thrusts to yourself with your hands (D) or use a blunt projection – for example, a tree stump or, if you are indoors, the back of a chair.

UNCONSCIOUS VICTIM

Place the heel of one of your hands against the middle of his or her abdomen, just above the navel. Place the other hand on top, and press with a quick upward thrust. If the obstacle is not freed, try removing it with a finger or an instrument such as a pair of forceps or tweezers. Use a torch, if necessary, to examine the upper airway. If the victim stays unconscious, call for help. If there is no breathing, use artificial respiration.

INFANT

Straddle the baby over your arm with the head below the level of the rest of the body. Support the baby's head by holding its jaw. Give the baby four

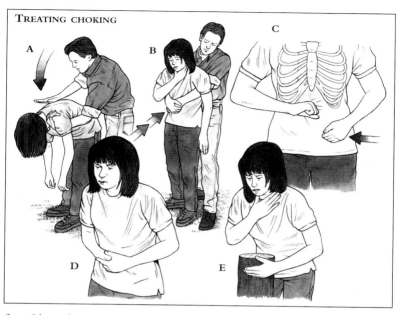

TREATING CHOKING

firm blows between the shoulder blades, taking care not to damage its spine or bruise it.

NEAR DROWNING

Signs of near drowning include:

- Pale and cool skin
- No breathing
- Blue lips (cyanosis)
- Weak or absent pulse
- Unconsciousness

Check that their airway is clear of any debris, false teeth and so on, and check for a pulse. Start CPR – Cardio-Pulmonary Resuscitation, if the victim has no pulse. Treat the victim for any signs of hypothermia and shock. It is vital that you keep the head lower than the rest of the body in order to allow water to drain naturally from the lungs. If the patient is coughing and spluttering, turn him/her on their side. If he/she is unconscious, use the recovery position (see page 257). Then call for medical assistance.

138. HOW TO TREAT BLEEDING

Severe loss of blood will lead to shock (see below). Bleeding can be arterial, venous or capillary, in order of seriousness.

- **Arterial**
  Blood in the arteries is under high pressure. If an artery is ruptured, the victim is in danger of a fatal loss of blood, and could die within minutes. Arterial blood can be recognized by its bright red colour and by the spurting effect that flows in time with the pumping of the heart.

- **Venous**
  Venous blood is more easily controlled than arterial blood, and is a darker shade of red.

- **Capillary**
  The blood vessels opened in minor cuts and grazes.

SEVERE WOUNDS

First of all, apply direct pressure to the wound in order to stop the flow of blood. You will need to allow enough time for the wound to seal itself. Apply a sterile dressing with firm pressure to control the bleeding. I bleeding continues, do not remove the first dressing, but add other dressings on top. If there is no fracture or dislocation, try to raise the limb that has been wounded and support it.

Another, less effective way of controlling bleeding is by using pressure points to seal off an artery above the wound. You should apply pressure at the end of the joint just above the injured area. On the hands, feet and head, this will be the wrist, ankle and neck respectively.

CUTS AND GRAZES

If there is a slight cut, try to rinse the wound in clean water to remove any grit or dirt. Dab it gently with sterile gauze to dry it and apply a dressing.

INTERNAL BLEEDING

Signs of internal bleeding may include frothy, bright-red blood coughed up by the victim (indicating bleeding in the lungs) or red blood in vomit (indicating bleeding in the stomach). Internal bleeding may be less obvious than external bleeding. You can make deductions about what is likely to have resulted internally from the type of accident the victim has suffered or the areas of bruising or tenderness.

Other signs and symptoms of internal bleeding include:

- Pale, clammy skin
- Rapid and weak pulse
- Rapid, shallow breathing
- Tenderness in the abdomen
- Any pain or discomfort
- Nausea and/or vomiting
- Shock

If you suspect internal bleeding, lay the victim down with their legs elevated and their knees bent. Remember, all a person's blood can be lost in the body cavities. Call for medical assistance. Do not give anything by mouth.

WOUNDS

Open wounds need to be treated with great care in a survival situation because of the danger of contamination and the difficulties in keeping things clean. Remove any clothing from around the wound, by cutting it away if necessary. Clean the skin round the wound and irrigate the wound to remove any dirt. Cover it with a clean dressing, which should be changed daily to check for infection.

If the wound does become infected, place a warm moist compress on it and hold it there for 30 minutes. Allow the wound to drain. Then dress and bandage the wound again. If maggots get in the wound, you can leave them for as long as they are feeding on dead tissue. Pain and redness indicate that they have begun to feed on live tissue, in which case the maggots should be flushed out with sterile water or urine.

GENERAL RULES FOR APPLYING DRESSINGS

The dressing pad should always extend well beyond the wound's edges. Place dressings directly on a wound. Do not slide them from the side, and replace any that slip out of place.

If blood seeps through a dressing, do not remove it; instead, apply another dressing over the top. If there is only one sterile dressing, use this to cover the wound, and use other materials as top dressings.

APPLYING STERILE DRESSINGS

Remove the wrapping. Unwind the bandage's loose end, taking care not to drop the roll or touch the dressing pad. Unfold the dressing pad, holding the bandage on each side of the pad. Put the pad directly on the wound. Wind the short end of the bandage once around the limb and the dressing to secure the pad. Then leave it hanging.

Wind the other end of the bandage around the limb to cover the whole pad, leaving the tail hanging free.

To secure the bandage, tie the ends in a reef knot, tied over the pad to exert firm pressure on the wound. Check the circulation to the extremity of the injured limb. Loosen the bandage if necessary.

ADHESIVE DRESSING

If it is a gaping wound, you can use adhesive tape cut in the closure form of a butterfly clip to bring the sides of the wound together. Ensure the wound is thoroughly clean and sterile before closure. If necessary, and if you have confidence and training, you can use sutures.

139. STITCHING A WOUND

Ensure there are no pockets of air or blood left below the skin. Make sure all materials used are clean. Pass the needle into one edge of the skin, through the full depth of the wound and out of the other edge. Knot each stitch at one side. Take in equal amounts of skin on both sides to align the edges of the wound.

Tie the sutures with a square knot. Loop over the needle holder, grasp the end through the loop and pull tight; loop round the needle holder in the opposite direction, grasp the end through the loop and pull tight again.

You should leave the sutures in place for about ten days. When you

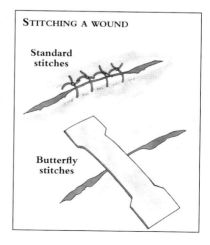

STITCHING A WOUND

Standard stitches

Butterfly stitches

take them out, grasp the knot with forceps and tweezers and pull the stitch out with a firm pull.

140. TREATING BURNS

In a survival situation, burns, especially if they are serious, can be among the most traumatic of wounds to treat. Whatever their cause, burns can inflict great pain and damage on the human body.

The dangers of receiving burns are possibly greater in a survival or outdoor scenario than in a domestic situation. Surviving in the open often involves open and hand-tended fires, tins of boiling water balanced on a small primus stove, and the carriage of various mechanisms and fuel for producing fire and heat.

From the first-aider's point of view, burns can cover the full spectrum of emergency challenge. At one end of the scale, there are the minor burns we have all encountered – touching a hot cooking pot, a slight rope burn, contact with the end of a cigarette. At the other end of the scale are full-depth burns covering a high percentage of the casualty's body. These may not only cause direct heat and flame damage, but also have life-threatening repercussions through fluid loss and ancillary injuries such as smoke inhalation.

The other thing to remember is that treating serious burns can be a psychologically disturbing experience. The casualty may be screaming with the great pain that often accompanies burns, and the sight and smell of scorched flesh can be particularly nauseating. Ideally, attend a first-aid training centre where burns injuries are replicated using make-up. This will not have the authenticity of the real thing, but adjusting to the sight of it will be excellent training should you have to deal with a serious burn in real life.

TYPES OF BURN

Burns have many different and diverse causes, all resulting in injury when destructive levels of heat come in contact with a point on the human body.

BURNS

TYPE OF BURN	DAMAGE	TREATMENT
First-degree	Top layer of skin, e.g. sunburn. Skin turns red and then peels off.	Rehydrating creams. Treatment for restlessness, headache or fever – cool water at regular intervals.
Second-degree	Deeper damage to the skin, causing blisters. Shock.	Use antibacterial dressing, or leave wound undressed but kept scrupulously clean. Treatment for shock.
Third-degree	Damage to all layers of skin. Shock.	Requires specialist treatment.

In fact, the list of burn causes is surprisingly broad, and goes well beyond contact with flame. The main types of burns in an outdoor survival situation are:

- Dry burn – contact with a direct dry heat source such as a flame, hotplate or cigarette.
- Friction burn – burn caused by heat build-up through friction, most commonly a rope burn.
- Sunburn – over-exposure to the sun's ultra-violet rays.
- Scald – caused by high-temperature liquid or steam.
- Cold burn – often not considered a burn, but frostbite or contact with

freezing metals of substances can cause burn injuries.

- Electrical burn – less common in the outdoors, but still possible from sources such as lightning or overhead pylons.
- Chemical burns – can come from acid or alkali substances, and a wide variety of industrial chemicals.
- Respiratory burns – burns to the mouth, nose, windpipe, or lungs through the inhalation of superheated air or caustic gases.

TREATMENT

Cool the area with water, or snow for 10–20 minutes or use a burn gel. Make the victim as comfortable as possible, protecting the wound from dirt. Do not remove anything that is sticking to the burn.

Do not apply lotions, ointments, butter or fat to the injury. Provide adequate fluid for the victim to drink, then get help as soon as possible.

Regularly check the person's vital signs, especially if the burns are serious.

141. LANCING A BLISTER

Blisters are a form of friction injury that needs special consideration. This is not only because they are so tremendously common, but also because if they are left untreated and in insanitary conditions for long, they can produce serious infections.

Prevention of foot blisters, the most common form of blister, is possible through changing socks regularly, wearing properly-fitted boots and performing organized foot checks on a walk. Blisters will announce themselves by producing a recognizable hot spot on your skin, and this is the moment at which you should take action with a change of footwear or socks. If an ointment is available, it should be applied. Once the area has been cooled and treated, you can set off again.

Sometimes blisters will develop fully. Do not voluntarily burst them unless your mobility is affected. In this case, bursting should be applied

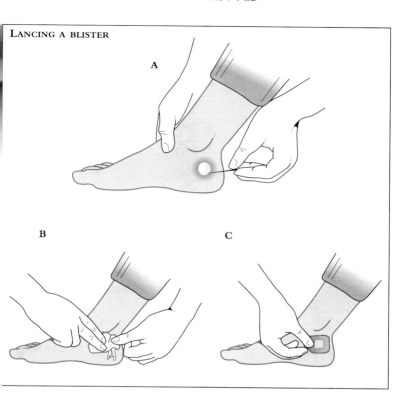

LANCING A BLISTER

A

B

C

through the following technique:

- Clean the area around the blister thoroughly using soap and water, which can act as a good enough disinfectant.
- You now need a sterilized needle or blade to lance the blister. Sterilize by immersing the steel in alcohol, boiling it for about 5 minutes, or

holding it over a flame. Even better is to have sterilized needles sealed away in your medical pack.

- Pierce the blister at one end, usually its lowest point, and allow the fluid to drain out. Do not pull away the blister skin. Instead, let it stay there to protect the wound from infection.

- Cover the wound and regularly clean it. Keep checking it for infection and apply some antibiotic ointment if you have it.

142. TREATING HYPERTHERMIA (HEATSTROKE)

Heatstroke and sunstroke (induced by direct sunlight) are life-threatening conditions requiring rapid emergency action. Once the casualty has reached this stage, their internal thermostat has failed, and the result of this damage can be coma and even death. It should also be noted that heatstroke is not only caused by environmental pressures, but can also be brought about by fevers or other illnesses which attack heat regulation.

Heatstroke shares many symptoms with heat exhaustion, but at a more severe level. Pulse and respiration may be racing and the casualty may drift in and out of consciousness. Skin may be either pale and clammy (though sweating usually has stopped) or very dry and hot. The most telling symptom will be given by a thermometer reading – their temperature will reach above 40°C (104°F).

Naturally, the most pressing priority here is the rapid cooling of the body. However, be careful. Do not plunge the person into a cold stream, river or other water source – this sudden chill may actually increase the body's core temperature through shock reaction and worsen matters, or the casualty's body temperature may reverse drastically and go into hypothermia. Immersion can be done later, and only for short controlled periods, after more appropriate initial cooling.

Initial cooling can be carried out by two methods, in both cases after removing the outer clothing:

● Strip the casualty down to their underclothes. Soak or spray them with water and then fan them to increase evaporation from the skin.

● Cover the casualty with a sheet, then soak this with water. Keep soaking the sheet to keep it cold. (If the case is very severe and death is likely, wait until the initial cooling begins to take effect, then fully immerse the body.) Do this slowly and massage the body continually to keep the circulation pumping out from the core of the body, thus accelerating heat loss. Remove immediately as temperature falls.

As these techniques are applied, keep diligently checking the vital signs. Especially watch the thermometer reading. Once this drops close to normal, you can stop the cooling, but be vigilant, as the temperature may climb once again. Also watch that the temperature does not fall dramatically, and always cover the casualty lightly to ensure that a chill does not set in.

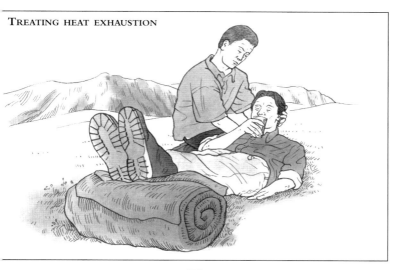

TREATING HEAT EXHAUSTION

Once the casualty returns to consciousness, perform the same process of rehydration demanded of heat exhaustion above. Keep checking the vital signs, and move them out of any wet clothes and into dry ones. The casualty still needs urgent evacuation at this point. Heatstroke can inflict serious brain damage or other complications, so professional medical control is essential.

143. TREATING HYPOTHERMIA (EXPOSURE)

Hypothermia is the condition in which the body's core temperature drops below 35°C (95°F). It is usually caused by excessive exposure to cold, wet and windy weather conditions, or from immersion in cold water. Except in extreme situations, such as when the casualty has been submerged in icy waters, it can be very difficult to diagnose; hypothermia can build up over hours as well as suddenly in minutes. A person with mild hypothermia will probably have perfectly normal blood pressure, pulse and respiration. Yet there are still clear indications which should give cause for concern. Mentally, the person may suffer from sudden, dramatic swings of mood and energy level, lack of concentration, and a tendency to withdraw. Physically they may look pale, with bouts of intense shivering, and their hands and legs may become less agile as the body draws blood away from the surface to the major organs.

At this point, take the person's temperature. This should preferably be done rectally, as the cooling of the extremities may lead to an inaccurate reading from the mouth or armpit. If the thermometer reads 32–35°C (90–95°F), you should immediately start to treat for mild hypothermia:

● Place the casualty in a position sheltered from wind and rain. Break their contact with the cold ground by placing insulation beneath them.
● Make sure that they are warm and dry. Change their wet clothing if possible (one item at a time to avoid total body exposure to the ele-

ments), and wrap them in a blanket or other protective layer. Non-breathable wraps, such as plastic sheets or thermal blankets, can stop further evaporative cooling.

● Next, move them to sources of warmth. This could be a fire or even other people – shared body warmth through hugging will treat them and protect you.

● Get them to eat and drink suitable foods. Do not do this if they are unconscious.

If all these techniques are applied consistently, then mild hypothermia can be reversed quite successfully. Success will be confirmed with the return to a normal temperature level and a better mental state, but keep monitoring all vital signs.

Mild hypothermia, if left untreated or overlooked, can ultimately lead to severe hypothermia when the body's core temperature dips below 33°C (91°F). This requires a different level of consideration than mild hypothermia as the symptoms are quite distinct and the urgency is that much greater. Forms of mental derangement may be apparent, and shivering can cease as the body runs out of energy. From there, the casualty can make the steady descent into unconsciousness.

DEALING WITH UNCONSCIOUSNESS

If they do descend into unconsciousness, be careful that you do not misinterpret this as death (although you should also be aware that death is not very far away at this point). Death is an easy misdiagnosis, as both pulse and respiration may be almost entirely undetectable in a hypothermic casualty, and their complexion will be icy and cold. To be on the safe side in this situation, start the warming process, and see if you get any response from the vital signs.

● Wrap the patient in warming layers (or place them in a good sleeping

TREATING HYPOTHERMIA

bag), and also a waterproof layer such as a tent ground sheet, in order to prevent any further evaporation cooling. Apply direct warming using whatever is to hand, such as thermal packs, water bottles, and heated and wrapped stones. Apply these to the armpits and wrists, the back of neck and small of back, the pit of the stomach and between the thighs. These are all places that have blood supply very near the surface and this blood, when warmed, will travel more directly to the body core.

- Evacuation is absolutely imperative for a person in this condition. However, move the person with care, as their heart muscle is in poor condition. Keep the casualty flat at all times, as this will ensure that the main blood reserves are kept in the core. Be prepared to resuscitate.

Severe hypothermia is a very serious predicament for the casualty and survival chances can be slim. Do not give up trying, however, particularly if your patient has been recovered after a long time in freezing water.

In fact, the shock of water-induced hypothermia can send the person's body into a kind of suspension, in which the body actually demands less and less oxygen, and so can be revived, even after all vital signs are gone.

144. TREATING FROSTBITE (AND FROSTNIP)

Frostbite is defined as the freezing of skin and tissue in sub-zero temperatures. It generally attacks the extremities of the body, which are most often deprived of blood flow in cold weather. These are the feet and toes, the hands, and most areas of the face, in particular the nose and ears.

FROSTNIP

The first degree of frostbite is known as frostnip, a thoroughly treatable condition that is nonetheless a forecast of possible frostbite. Frostnip occurs when there is a freezing in the skin's outermost layers. The symptoms are pins and needles in the affected area, followed by a change to numbness. The skin colour will be white or grey (in light-skinned people) or pink (in dark-skinned people) and somewhat waxy, very cold to the touch. Reverse this condition by simply rewarming.

Place hands, for instance, in warm spots such as the armpits or groin; in the case of other extremities, someone else may have to apply body heat or another heat source in the best way available. When the skin becomes slightly red and swollen, with the casualty feeling some pain and discomfort, the treatment has been successful. Keep an eye on someone who has been treated for frostnip, as those areas of the body affected are more prone to refreezing.

TREATMENT FOR FROSTBITE

If the freezing goes beyond frostnip, the symptoms become steadily more alarming, and more sensitivity of treatment is required.

As frostbite advances, the skin will become hard and rigid; patches of tough swelling appear and these can then blister; the colours of the skin go from pale to a variegated blue, and then finally black as the tissue is frozen solid and infected. In these final stages, the frostbitten area will feel exactly like a piece of meat taken from a freezer, and the casualty will find it impossible to move. (Do not try to manipulate any frozen area – think what happens if you bend a frozen sausage). Ultimately, the blackened, blistered areas fall off as dead tissue.

A primary treatment for frostbite is to make sure that the person as a whole is warm and well clothed; get the person to eat and drink to maintain warmth levels from energy production. Remove any articles of clothing or jewellery that may be restricting blood flow to the area. For the frostbite itself, the best treatment would be delivered in the controlled conditions of a hospital. This is because infection can all too easily occur in insanitary outdoor conditions, and there is still the risk of refreezing, which would greatly compound the damage. Thus, if rescue is possible in a few hours, simply cover and protect the site with a dry gauze bandage and wait for the professionals.

If this is not going to be possible for some time, then steady rewarming of the casualty is the priority. Immerse the affected part of the body in warm water – elbow hot, but not uncomfortably hot, about 28°C/82°F – and keep it there while adding enough hot water to keep the temperature constant. The goal is to rewarm the frozen tissue. Always be careful about overheating, and if the casualty's pain starts to become especially severe, this may indicate an over-rapid rewarming.

Once rewarming has been achieved, prohibit the casualty's further use of the affected part and cover it lightly with a bandage. Splinting and elevating physical areas such as frozen hands is also recommended, as the rewarmed tissue is extremely fragile. Ibuprofen tablets taken according to dosage are an excellent anti-inflammatory. These are useful in stopping blood clots forming in the tissue, and also for controlling the pain that results from a rewarmed frostbitten area or digit. There are two things that you should never do to a frostbitten area: 1) Never rub the area; and 2) never burst any blisters that form.

Frostbite is a difficult condition to treat when outdoors; when the condition is advanced, you should generally prioritize rescue over treatment.

145. TREATING ANAPHYLACTIC SHOCK

Anaphylactic shock results when the body has a major allergic reaction to a foreign substance. Insect stings, the ingestion of certain food types, or contact with certain drugs are the most common cause of this reaction, but the effect is the same: the blood vessels dilate, causing pooling of blood and lack of circulatory blood volume, while the muscles and body tissue swell, often restricting or even closing the airway.

Sometimes anaphylaxis can take time to develop, but in other cases, it will take effect in seconds. The casualty will become distressed, the face will swell, and red blotches will start to appear on the skin. More seriously, breathing will become disrupted and laboured, and the pulse will increase. Unconsciousness can quickly follow.

The best treatment for anaphylaxis follows if the person is aware of their allergy and carries a syringe kit containing epinephrine, a manufactured

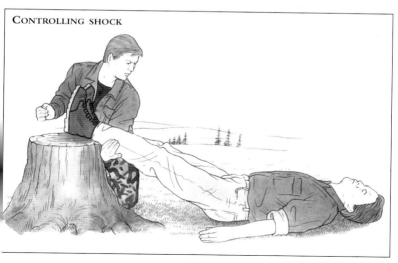

CONTROLLING SHOCK

from of adrenaline. This may well contain instructions for its application, especially with an Epipen which delivers the right dosage. Pharmacy-bought antihistamines can be used as an addition to lessen the effects of anaphylaxis. Indeed, epinephrine can wear off and the anaphylaxis appear again; using an antihistamine can prevent this.

If you are in an environment such as the tropics, where you may encounter many unfamiliar biting and stinging insects, it is possible that an unknown anaphylactic reaction can occur. General treatments for anaphylaxis are simply placing the casualty in a position in which they can breathe easily and, importantly, removing the source of the allergic reaction, such as pulling out the bee sting. Anaphylaxis is an acute reaction, so be diligent in taking away any items of the casualty's clothing that may contain traces of the allergy-inducing substance. As always with circulatory and respiratory disorders, be prepared to deliver resuscitation and keep a close eye on the casualty's vital signs.

146. FIXING BROKEN BONES

Bones can be broken in a simple fall. A closed, or simple, fracture is where the broken bone ends remain beneath the skin. An open, or compound, fracture is where both ends of the bone protrude through the skin.

Look for swelling, deformity or projecting bone ends, and severe pain that is made worse by movement.

TREATMENT

Do not try to force the bones back together again, but seek medical assistance. Treat all open wounds with a clean dressing.

Splint the fractured area in exactly the position that you find it in, pending removal to hospital or the arrival of expert medical aid. If the arm is fractured, splint it, and then set up a sling if the arm can be moved across the chest. Do not move the victim at all if you suspect a spinal injury.

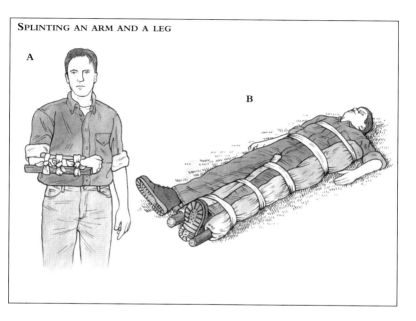

SPLINTING AN ARM AND A LEG

A

B

SPLINTS

You can use sticks, ski poles, ice axes, tree branches, boards or even a rolled newspaper to make a splint – in fact, anything that is rigid enough! The splint should be long enough to immobilize the limb above and below the fracture. Ensure the limb and splint are tied at four points, two above and two below the fracture. Tie the splint with non-slip knots, with the knot on the outside.

Make sure that the splint is adequately padded anywhere it touches a bony part of the body, otherwise it will be uncomfortable for the victim. You may tie the wounded limb to another part of the victim's body – for example, a wounded leg tied to a healthy leg, or a wounded arm to the chest. Place a splint on each side of the limb. When tying the splints on, make sure the bandages are tight enough to prevent the splints from slipping, but not so tight as to impede circulation.

Actual splinting techniques vary with each wound, but there is a general procedure to follow:

- Splint only a limb that has been aligned or, in the case of a joint, set to the mid-range position.
- Bind the stabilizer (or stabilizers – one on either side if required) to the broken limb so that the joints either side of the break are immobilized. For example, if the forearm is broken, the splint should also hold the elbow and the wrist. Run a padded stabilizer down the length of the limb and tie it in place with the bandages. Be careful with the tying so that you are not restricting circulation – check the colour of the skin and nails in the extremities for signs of infarction (dead tissue resulting from obstruction of the blood supply).
- If necessary for added stability, bind the splinted limb to an uninjured part of the body. Thus a splinted right leg could be tied to the left leg, or a broken arm tied to the torso. When doing this, however, make sure that there is plentiful padding in between the two body parts.

Once the fractured or dislocated limb is aligned and securely stabilized, the casualty is ready for evacuation. Maintain a close vigilance over the circulatory situation in the damaged area, and also watch for signs of any localized or systemic infection developing.

For stable fractures, the treatment can be modified, as often the casualty may still have use of the limb, with pain being possibly the only complication. Splint and support the broken limb, but also use cold compresses to bring down swelling. Then, if possible, elevate the fracture site.

Once the wound is stabilized and if you have the tools and natural materials around you, then it is possible to make improvised crutches to give the casualty some level of mobility. However, make sure that you know what you are doing – badly made crutches can lead to the casualty re-injuring himself if they break or bend suddenly.

CIRCULATION

It is important to check the circulation below the point of injury before tying on the splints. If there is no circulation in this area for too long, the limb may have to be amputated.

If the skin is pale or bluish in colour, this may indicate damage to an artery. You can also check by pressing down fingernails into the skin and watching how quickly the colour returns (this is known as capillary return). Check this by comparing with an uninjured extremity. Also check the temperature of the limb against another limb.

Check for circulation again after tying on the splints. Damaged arteries require urgent medical attention.

SLING

This can be made from non-stretching cloth or even a belt. The sling should place pressure on the uninjured side of the body and the hand should be slightly higher than the elbow when put in place across the body.

TYING A SLING

NECK FRACTURE

The neck should be immobilized with a cervical collar. Alternatively, place a rolled towel or cloth under the neck to support it and two weighted objects on either side of the head to keep it stable until help arrives.

FRACTURED RIBS

A fractured rib causes severe pain, which is worsened by deep breathing. Strapping is rarely used for a rib injury because of the difficulty of maintaining breathing with a strap in place. The victim should be encouraged to hold the injured side while taking deep breaths. There is a danger that a fractured rib might pierce a lung. The signs of this may include difficulty in breathing, skin turning a blue colour (cyanosis) and shock. Get urgent medical help.

SKULL FRACTURE

Most skull fractures are closed and do not create complications. A severe injury may cause bone fragments to be forced inwards, rupturing the

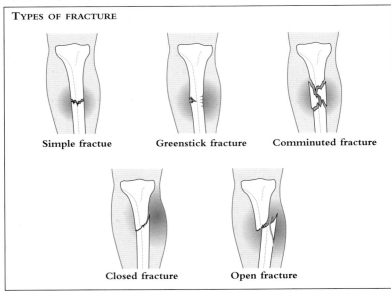

TYPES OF FRACTURE

Simple fractue Greenstick fracture Comminuted fracture

Closed fracture Open fracture

blood vessels of the membrane covering the brain. The blood clot that results may press onto brain tissue.

If there is straw-coloured fluid seeping from an ear or the nose, this may indicate rupture of the brain membrane blood vessels by a fracture of the base of the skull. The victim should be put in the recovery position, allowing any fluid to run out. Call for urgent medical assistance.

147. TREATING A DISLOCATED SHOULDER

A dislocated shoulder occurs when the ball-and-socket joint of the arm bone and the shoulder socket become displaced. This occurs usually after a fall or wrenching injury. Symptoms are distortion, swelling and pain in the area, as well as a 'flattening' of the shoulder's general appearance. Dislocation will also result in a loss of mobility in the respective limb, and circulatory restrictions resulting from this injury can be acute.

Do not attempt to manipulate the bones back into position unless you have had First Aid training. Instead, make a sling in order to prevent movement. Call for medical assistance.

If you have First Aid training, act quickly before the muscles around the joint begin to tighten up. Apply traction or pull the joint, then move the attached limb in the direction that it would normally move. Release the traction or pulling force and check for nerve response. If a nerve is pinched, repeat the procedure. Apply cold packs to reduce the swelling.

Traction techniques for relocating a dislocated shoulder can be tricky, mainly because of the muscular strength in the upper body. Use whichever of the following two techniques lends itself to the situation:

A particularly effective technique is as follows. Lie the casualty down on a patch of ground, and gently apply traction to the injured arm, pulling with one arm gripping above the elbow. Maintaining the traction, bring the casualty's arm up to about a 90° angle from their body, bend at the elbow and rotate the arm upwards until the final position is

APPLYING DOWNWARD TRACTION

like someone holding a ball ready for throwing. Hold this position and the traction for up to 10 minutes while the muscles in the shoulder slowly relax. This in itself will usually allow the joint to slip back into place. If not, then watch for a specific moment of relaxation and rotate the arm steadily forward, as if the hand was now 'throwing the ball'. This should relocate the joint.

Another method of relocation is to make the casualty lay face down on an elevated surface with the arm of the injured shoulder hanging over the side. Take hold of the dangling arm, and maintain downward traction for about 15–20 minutes. Once you gently let go, the shoulder should relocate itself.

Once the joint is relocated, the arm on the injured side should be stabilized in an arm sling. Take a large piece of material and, starting from the uninjured shoulder, wrap it underneath the arm with the material supporting from the fingertips to past the elbow joint, then tie the loose ends behind the neck or across the chest.

148. TREATING SPRAINS, STRAINS AND BRUISES

Sprains, strains, and bruises are the everyday hazard of the enthusiast of outdoor pursuits. But though common, they can also be extremely debilitating injuries and if incurred in an unforgiving environment, they may become dangerous.

Though sprains, strains and bruises can happen to many different parts of the body, there is a standard procedure for treatment. This procedure is also applicable for stable fractures and is commonly known as the RICE procedure:

Rest the injured part
Ice the injured part – chill the wound with an ice pack or cold compress
Compress the injury
Elevate the injured part

This four-stage procedure can dramatically reduce the swelling that commonly accompanies these types of injuries.

The procedure is explained below by referring to a sprained ankle, but the same could be used for any limb or bruised area of the body. Severe bruising on body regions other than the limbs naturally means that elevation is unlikely to be an option.

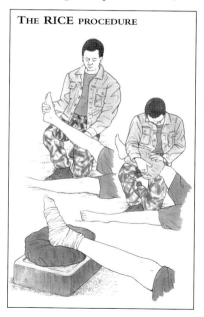

THE **RICE** PROCEDURE

- Take the casualty's twisted ankle, and immediately elevate, while applying a cold compress directly to the injury for about 10–15 minutes.
- Wrap the ankle in an elasticized bandage or some other compressive bandaging – this compression will also help to reduce swelling. However, check that the compression is not too tight, and release it briefly every hour to aid circulation. Keep the ankle

raised in this recovery position.

- Give ibuprofen or other anti–inflammatory and painkilling drugs as needed and according to the instructions and only if you are qualified to administer such drugs.
- If it is considered necessary, for a bad sprain or strain, the ankle or any limb can be splinted in order to provide extra healing support to the affected area.

A slightly more problematic situation is that of inflamed tendons, ligaments, and muscles. This usually happens as a result of over–activity and constant wear and tear. Inflammation is often associated with those activities that involve regular motions such as canoeing, walking and skiing. Rest is actually what is needed, but this, of course, is not always possible.

The treatment above is still relevant to this type of injury, though it is the warming treatments that will provide the most beneficial help unless there is an immediate swelling. Most importantly, try to alter the way in which the casualty does his activity, or the length of time he spends doing it. This will help to give the injured area a rest from the affective movement that is causing the problem.

With all the procedures outlined above – but particularly in the case of fractures and dislocations – do not try to perform the treatments if you are not sure of what you are doing. Steer well clear of certain treatments that may appear natural, such as massaging a sprained joint, which does little good and may actually encourage inflammation.

As with all First Aid procedures, prior training is invaluable for handling these situations successfully, so make the investment before you travel.

149. TREATING KNEE INJURIES

In survival situations, an injured knee will affect your ability to move from your present location. This could be a major problem if movement is

IMPROVISED CRUTCHES

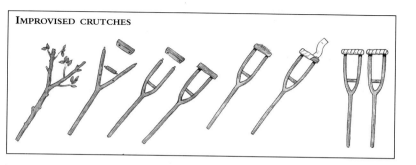

essential to your survival. Stabilization and support will be required.

Injuries to the knee can occur in many different ways owing to the complexity of the physical structure. Most vulnerable are the patella, or kneecap, and the ligaments that connect the femur, tibia and fibula bones. Any violent twisting motion, a blow to the knee or imposing too much pressure on the knee, can displace the kneecap, or tear or strain the ligaments. The primary symptoms of either of these injuries are joint pain, knee immobility and a localized swelling of the knee joint.

Dislocated kneecaps can often be relocated, and this should be attempted if there will be a wait of more than two hours for professional help. Have the casualty sit up and then gently try to straighten the leg. The knee cap may pop in of its own accord as you do this, or you can try giving it a guiding push with your thumb. However, if the leg does not want to straighten or the pain is too intense for the casualty, do not attempt to force it. If you have managed to relocate the kneecap, splint the joint for stability. Try not to let the casualty walk on the knee for some time, as this can often result in a re-dislocation.

For injuries to the knee, such as torn ligaments or crushing injuries, then it is best simply to place the knee in the least painful position before stabilizing.

150. ALL THE OTHER THINGS THAT COULD GO WRONG!

Most domestic and workplace first aid deals with the immediate treatment of accidents or rapid-effect illnesses such as anaphylaxis. The range of medical challenges encountered by the survival first-aider can be substantially broader.

This is principally because there is a wide range of illnesses worldwide that thrive on the unsanitary conditions often encountered outdoors. Furthermore, these illnesses are able to gain a substantial hold as professional medical care is usually far away. The care of a doctor is exactly what is needed if a person falls ill in the wilderness – First Aid can only go so far when modern medicines and medical procedures are required. In the absence of professional medical staff on your team, you should be aware that rescue or evacuation is usually the end goal of your treatment.

Many of the diseases and illnesses that follow are infectious, so exercise a rigorous hygiene policy around the sick person.

- If necessary, isolate the casualty from the group.
- Sterilize any utensils used by the patient before they are used by anyone else in the group.
- Be sure to avoid all contact with the patient's body fluids or waste – even the output produced when the patient coughs.
- Be diligent about disposing of the patient's body waste well away from your camp; preferably, bury it.

As a first-aider, your job is not to cure complex diseases, but to get the casualty safely to professional medical care. Always remember this rule: if you do not know what illness you're dealing with – even the professionals can be unsure – do not make a snap diagnosis. Instead, respond only to those symptoms you understand, such as dehydration and respiratory problems, and deal with these while accepting you do not know the root cause. This is all that can be expected of you.

APPENDICITIS/PERITONITIS AND ABDOMINAL PROBLEMS

Your appendix is attached to the lower intestine below, and to the right of, your navel. It serves no significant purpose in the body, but if it becomes infected, the consequences can be serious. Once infected, it swells, causing great pain and illness, and can eventually burst and cause peritonitis – infection of the peritoneum, the membranous sack which contains the human organs. This is a life-threatening situation.

The symptoms of appendicitis begin with a general abdominal pain focused around the navel, which becomes increasingly severe and extends downwards to the lower right side. The pain may be accompanied by fever, vomiting and constipation. Further diagnosis can be made by using the rebound test. Position your fingers a little way above the left groin and press down. When the casualty reports that this is beginning to hurt, quickly remove your hand. If a harsh pain hits the casualty when you remove your hand, then appendicitis or peritonitis are the likely causes. If peritonitis is the case, the severity of the illness will increase and the abdomen will become rock hard and very painful to touch.

In either case, surgery will be necessary, so evacuate (using a stretcher) or quickly arrange a rescue. Your first treatment will largely be preventative – do not let the person ingest food or drink. However, if dehydration becomes a problem, administer sips of water.

CHOLERA

Cholera is a gastro-intestinal infection caused by ingesting water infected with the vibrio cholerae bacterium. Cholera occurs wherever there are unsanitary conditions, and travellers to any developing countries must have a cholera vaccine in advance. Those who die of cholera, as many do worldwide, usually die of chronic dehydration through violent and prolonged diarrhoea. The fluid loss is dramatic. Other symptoms include low blood pressure, muscle pain, fever and shock. Cholera requires hospitalization as soon as possible, but in the meantime, all you can do is give the generic treatment for dehydration (see Diarrhoea below), but with the drinks given almost constantly. One of the problems facing the survival first-aider is disposing of the waste produced by the cholera patient. If possible, try to improvise some form of latrine over which the casualty can be positioned.

CRAMP

Cramp occurs when chemicals build up in the muscle, often in association with physical exercise when the participant sweats a great deal. It is a common problem for those on outdoor pursuits, and the strong muscular spasms that cramp induces can disable a limb for many minutes if not treated. Cramp usually affects the legs. For a thigh cramp, elevate the casualty's leg, then straighten it if the cramp is on the back of the thigh and bend it if the cramp is on the front of the thigh. For cramp in the calf, straighten the knee again and bend the foot back towards the shin. For foot cramp, take the casualty's foot onto your knee, move it back and forth, and massage. Massage should be applied to the affected muscle in all cases. Cramp thus treated should pass away in a couple of minutes.

DIARRHOEA

It is often very difficult to pin down the causes of diarrhoea. Food poisoning, change in climate, infection and overeating can all cause diarrhoea. In most cases, the complaint will clear up in a few hours or, at most, a couple of days. If the diarrhoea persists and the condition is acute, dehydration becomes a serious threat. To counter dehydration, focus on rehydrating the casualty with half a teaspoon of salt and eight teaspoons of sugar mixed into 1 litre (1¾ pints) of water. Administer the water in frequent sips, but do not give any food for 24 hours. After this period, give nutritious food (nothing greasy, spicy or alcoholic, and avoid raw fruit initially). Soups and broths are the ideal introductory foods; then proceed onto cooked vegetables and plain, well-cooked meats.

HAEMORRHOIDS (PILES)

A haemorrhoid results from a clot or mass building up in a vein around the rim of the anus. This swells outward to create small external lumps that can bleed, sometimes profusely enough to warrant surgery. Haemorrhoids are caused in several different ways, most commonly by anal infections, through abdominal pressure such as that experienced when lifting heavy objects, or with constipation.

Outdoor adventurers can be vulnerable to piles because of the level of exertion on the body. For those who are aware of their condition, suppositories and medications are available. In a wilderness situation, the best treatment is to bathe the anus with warm water (preferably immerse the backside), and eat lots of fruit and fibrous foods to make stools looser and easier to pass. If a pile is bleeding, treat it like any other wound and apply direct pressure – take it seriously, as the bleeding is directly from a vein.

HEPATITIS

Hepatitis is an inflammation of the liver due to a variety of causes, and can be both infectious and non-infectious. It is usually transferred when the body waste of an infected person is passed into water or food, which is then ingested by another person. Sexual intercourse is also a primary route of infection. The main symptoms of hepatitis are lack of appetite, abdominal pain, vomiting, very dark urine and whitish stools, and a yellow tinge to skin and eyes several days after infection.

As hepatitis is a virus, antibiotics will not help. In fact, many medicines will simply damage the liver further. The casualty needs as much rest as possible, so camp down in one spot and bring rescuers in, rather than attempt to walk the casualty out. Give plenty of fluids and encourage ingestion of foods in fluid form, such as soups and fruit juice, which supply nutrients and energy. If the casualty can eat, feed them with fruit, vegetables, starches and proteins, but keep fats to a minimum, as the body will not tolerate them.

HERNIA

A hernia tends to occur suddenly when a person is lifting something heavy or doing a task that requires strenuous exertion. A hernia is actually a rupture of the muscle wall in the abdomen, allowing a piece of intestine to bulge through. This bulge is noticeable and is usually, but not always, in the lower groin. It can be distinguished from the lymph nodes in this region by the fact that it will increase in size if the person lifts anything.

Hernias can be serious because the abdominal muscles may clamp the piece of intestine and actually block the movement of the bowels. This is an urgent situation requiring professional medical care as soon as possible. Symptoms include severe abdominal pain, vomiting (sometimes with faeces in the vomit) and stubborn constipation. If the casualty is suffering from this type of hernia (known as a 'strangulated' hernia, a surgical emergency), place in a comfortable position of their own choosing, and resist giving them anything to drink unless dehydration becomes a problem. Do not give any food at all. However, if the hernia is painless and not creating any inconvenience, there is no cause for alarm. Simply try to stop the person doing any heavy lifting or over-exerting themselves.

MALARIA AND DENGUE

Malaria and dengue are diseases spread by mosquitoes, so it is very important to take preventative precautions such as anti-malarial tablets, insect repellents and sleeping nets. It is also easy to confuse the symptoms of the two diseases.

Malaria causes feverish attacks that occur initially once a day, but then about once every two or three days. These attacks usually begin with chills and violent shivering, followed by a high fever that can last days, then a period of sweating and temperature subsidence. However, there are other types of malaria, which can result in coma and anaemia. Whatever the type, the only treatment for malaria, apart from generic treatments for fever, is medicinal. If you are travelling to any area known to have malaria, start a course of anti-malarial drugs before travelling, and maintain the course according to directions while you are there. If a member of your party gets malaria, then evacuate.

Dengue is also transmitted by mosquitoes and is also characterized by chills and fevers, though it is often accompanied by a rash that spreads from the extremities across the body. Dengue should cure itself and provide immunity after a few days, though some Southeast Asian strains can do more serious damage by inducing bleeding from the skin and internally. Rest and generic treatments for fever, bleeding and dehydration are the only recourse.

MENINGITIS

Meningitis is a chronic infection of the brain that can easily be fatal. It tends to be confined to children, but can also occur in adults, particularly following another infectious illness.

The symptoms of meningitis are fever and headache, combined with a painful sensitivity to light, a very stiff neck, vomiting, convulsions and a purple or red rash (the spots do not fade when you press your finger on them). The illness is very serious, and all you can do is to control any temperature imbalances and failures of major systems, while transporting the casualty to professional medical facilities as soon as possible.

POLIOMYELITIS

Poliomyelitis is a disease that can cause paralysis by attacking the nerve cells in the spinal cord responsible for motor impulses. It invades orally, but not everyone who contracts it becomes ill; sometimes they will just experience a mild fever.

However, when the attack is more serious, the symptoms are very much like those of meningitis – severe headache, photophobia (aversion to light), a stiff neck and vomiting. The casualty either gets better or worsens, developing paralysis in certain parts of the body. Naturally, by this stage, evacuation proceedings should have been instigated by the first-aider. There is little you can do in the way of treatment. Place hot packs on the muscles to keep them warm. Move the paralysed limbs around to avoid muscular deterioration. Watch carefully for any signs of respiratory distress developing and react accordingly.

RABIES

Rabies is a lethal disease that attacks the central nervous system following infection. The infection itself is transmitted through the bite of an infected animal, such as a dog, cat or bat. A rabid animal can be identified by such traits as foaming at the mouth, an alternately violent, disturbed and lethargic temperament, and death within a week. If a person has been bitten, clean the bite thoroughly with soap and water.

The symptoms of rabies in humans are respiratory disturbances, pain in the bite area and throat, problems with swallowing, major personality swings, convulsions and paralysis (the last symptoms usually precede the casualty's death). These symptoms do not occur immediately but usually develop within two months of the bite. Your goal is quickly to move the casualty to a hospital or doctor.

TRENCH FOOT OR IMMERSION FOOT

This is caused by the exposure of feet to wet and damp conditions over a prolonged period. Feet will initially turn pale, with little detectable pulse, and later become red, swollen and painful, with a strong pulse. If the feet are at the stage where they are pale, warm them gently. Do not expose them to direct heat, as this can lead to gangrene (tissue death).

If the feet are at the stage where they are red and swollen, cool them down gradually. Do not massage the feet or apply direct heat. To prevent trench foot, ensure that socks are changed daily. You can keep up a rota of clean socks by tying a damp pair round your midriff where they will dry as you go about your activities.

TUBERCULOSIS

Tuberculosis (TB) is particularly concentrated in poor urban areas rather than rural settings, but the first-aider should be aware of it since it has an extremely contagious nature.

The age group most prone to catching tuberculosis is between 15 and 35. TB is primarily a lung disease, though it can actually affect any part of the body such as the neck and abdomen (it can also cause meningitis in children). It can be spread both by respiration and by drinking the milk from cattle with the bovine form of the disease. Symptoms are a severe cough that can contain significant amounts of blood in the later stage, fevers, chest and back pain, weight loss, fatigue and a hoarse voice.

Someone with TB needs to be taken to a doctor or hospital, and your main role as a first–aider is to stop the infection of others. Fashion a face mask that covers your nose and mouth, and wear it when dealing with the person. Keep other members of the group well away (observe them closely for signs of weight loss or coughing). Rest the casualty, and keep them warm and comfortable as much as the conditions allow.

TYPHOID

Typhoid is an infectious disease passed from faeces to food and water and then to a human host. Diligent hygiene and appropriate inoculation can make it almost entirely preventable. If it is contracted, it is very serious and requires immediate evacuation or rescue. Typhoid often emerges after natural disasters when sanitation breaks down, and usually comes in epidemics. In such situations, be especially diligent in purifying water and distinguishing suspect water or food supplies. Mark these as contaminated to warn others. Also set up latrine areas that are well away and distinct from habitation zones.

The symptoms are initially those of a bad cold or flu, but with a rising fever and, distinctively, a slowing pulse (good regular checks on the vital signs are required to spot this). There can also be vomiting and diarrhoea. After a week, other symptoms such as rash, delirium and weight loss can emerge. Coma and death can occur if left unchecked.

Your First Aid options are limited to general treatment of fever and dehydration until you can get the patient to hospital. Try also to give them nutritional liquids, such as fruit juices and soups. One final point is to remember that the casualty can be a typhoid carrier for some time after their recovery, so maintain the separation of their functions.

TYPHUS

Typhus is a similar illness to typhoid in symptoms and result, but it is spread by the bites of infected lice, ticks and rat fleas. Treatments are as for typhoid, but you should also make a great effort in your cleanliness regime, washing your body regularly to clean off lice. If you cannot move from a particular area, kill rats with traps and then burn the bodies (do not throw them in waterways, as their bodies will contaminate the water that may be used in developing countries for washing and even drinking).

YELLOW FEVER

Yellow fever is a mosquito-borne infection, which is present in areas of tropical Africa and South America. It takes its name from the jaundiced colour of the casualty following infection. Other symptoms include fever, headache, vomiting (often with a bloody content), constipation and reduced urination. Treatment for yellow fever consists of controlling the fever and dehydration elements of the illness, giving plenty of rest and allowing the illness to pass naturally. However, you should always initiate evacuation, as yellow fever can leave many complications.

SURVIVAL KITBAG

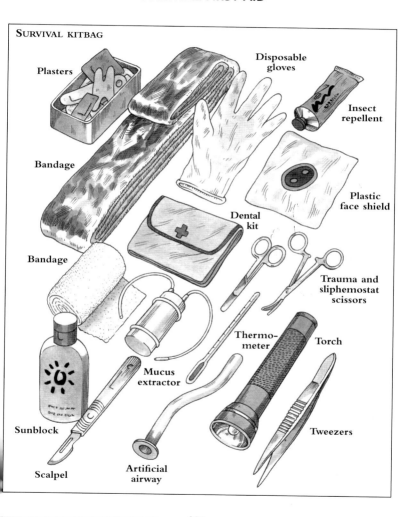

Plasters

Disposable gloves

Insect repellent

Bandage

Plastic face shield

Dental kit

Bandage

Trauma and sliphemostat scissors

Thermo-meter

Torch

Mucus extractor

Sunblock

Tweezers

Scalpel

Artificial airway

APPENDIX

Travel abroad demands plenty of preparation, even when going on a straight-forward trip to somewhere in North America or Europe. If you are travelling further afield you will not only need to carry out the standard checks for essential documents but also be aware of the potential problems and restrictions that could be caused by unstable political regimes, wars and inadequate emergency services. You should take care to respect local customs, especially with regard to accepted standards of dress. There may be a high risk of diseases such as malaria and cholera and you should always take care with local drinking water. Remember that in many countries you may be required to produce personal identification on the spot.

1. ASIA

This is the largest continent, with a total area of about 44,614,000 square km. It comprises the eastern four fifths of the Eurasian landmass. The Asian coastline is about 62,800 square km. It is the most highly populated continent at more than 3 billion, though large areas of central and north Asia have a relatively low population density.

AFGHANISTAN
Capital: Kabul

Travel tips: You should not travel to this country at all in the wake of the terrorist attacks on New York and Washington on September 11, 2001 and the subsequent military action.

ARMENIA
Capital: Yerevan

Travel tips: check on the current state of internal affairs; a visa is normally required; take care with regard to standard of driving in the country.

BANGLADESH
Capital: Dhaka
Travel tips: beware of dangers of organised crime and of the poor state of some roads.

BRUNEI
Capital: Bandar Seri Begawan
Travel tips: strict laws in place with regard to drugs.

BURMA
Capital: Rangoon
Travel tips: visitors are restricted to certain areas; do not photograph any kind of military installation; avoid large crowds/demonstrations; there are some dangers from the conflict between insurgents such as the Karen and the government.

CAMBODIA
Capital: Phnom Penh
Travel tips: beware of mines in some areas; avoid crowds/demonstrations; there can be severe floods in the rainy season.

CHINA
Capital: Beijing
Travel tips: there has been an increase in criminal activity and there is some unrest, due in part to ethnic discontent and rising unemployment. There is some danger of earthquakes.

GEORGIA
Capital: Tiblisi
Travel tips: a visa is normally required; some areas are dangerous; roads can be poor; take care with drinking water etc.

INDIA
Capital: New Delhi
Travel tips: disturbances in northeast and Kashmir should be avoided; beware confidence tricksters.

INDONESIA
Capital: Jakarta
Travel tips: check on latest political developments to gauge state of unrest.

IRAN
Capital: Tehran
Travel tips: dress modestly and take care to respect local customs in this regard; do not photograph military installations; ensure visa is valid.

IRAQ
Capital: Baghdad
Travel tips: do not visit unless given the all clear by your own government.

ISRAEL
Capital: Jerusalem
Travel tips: keep up to date with political developments which could affect travel plans; there have been bombs on public transport; carry identification at all times.

JAPAN
Capital: Tokyo
Travel tips: Japan is a high-risk earthquake area.

JORDAN
Capital: Amman
Travel tips: Although there is a peace treaty with Israel, there is much opposition to this in Jordan. Potential problems with terrorism mean that travellers should keep up to date with developments.

KAZAKHSTAN
Capital: Almaty (Alma Ata)
Travel tips: a visa is required; it is advisable for Westerners to travel in groups as they can be targets of robberies; travel to neighbouring states can be difficult.

KOREA, NORTH
Capital: P'yongyang
Travel tips: check on arrangements for representation by your government in this country.

KOREA, SOUTH
Capital: Seoul
Travel tips: obtain update on political developments as there is tension between North and South Korea which could erupt.

KUWAIT
Capital: Al Kuwayt
Travel tips: keep up to date with political developments, due to tensions with Iraq; keep away from Iraq border; take care with regard to unexploded shells, etc. which remain from the war.

LEBANON
Capital: Beirut
Travel tips: keep up to date with political developments in the region;

a visa is required; travel is restricted to certain areas, do not to photograph any military installations.

MALAYSIA
Capital: Kuala Lumpur
Travel tips: there are severe laws against drugs; keep away from crowds and demonstrations of any kind; respect local customs of decorum in dress, etc.

MONGOLIA
Capital: Ulaanbaatar (Ulan Bator)
Travel tips: entry into the country normally only by air and train; internal communications are poor.

NEPAL
Capital: Kathmandu
Travel tips: check on state of security of the region you are visiting; beware robberies; standard of driving and transport is poor; ensure you have all the correct insurance.

OMAN
Capital: Masqat (Muscat)
Travel tips: keep in touch with developments in the Middle East.

PAKISTAN
Capital: Islamabad
Travel tips: there is danger from armed gangs in some areas; travel can be risky; check on latest political developments and beware the tension with India over Kashmir.

PHILIPPINES
Capital: Manila
Travel tips: this is an earthquake and high-risk typhoon zone; carry identification; beware travelling alone in remote areas; beware of danger from malaria and take medical precautions.

RUSSIA
Capital: Moscow
Travel tips: check on advisability of travel in certain areas; there can be unrest caused by rival gangs; a visa is normally required.

SAUDI ARABIA
Capital: Riyadh
Travel tips: it is forbidden to import or use alcohol, religious material or pork; dress codes must be observed; check on the political status in the region.

SINGAPORE
Capital: Singapore City
Travel tips: there are strict drug laws; danger of offshore piracy.

SRI LANKA
Capital: Colombo
Travel tips: there have been bomb attacks; check on current state of tension between Tamil Tigers and security forces; do not photograph military installations; driving and roads are poor.

SYRIA
Capital: Dimasha (Damascus)
Travel tips: dress should respect local religious laws; no photography near military installations; a visa must be carried.

TAIWAN
Capital: T'ai-pei
Travel tips: beware dangers from earthquakes in this region.

THAILAND
Capital: Bangkok
Travel tips: drug laws are strictly enforced; beware dangers of flooding in some areas; do not travel to remote border areas without checking on the security situation.

TURKEY
Capital: Ankara
Travel tips: take comprehensive insurance; beware standard of driving is poor.

UNITED ARAB EMIRATES
Capital: Abu Dhabi
Travel tips: check on regional security before travel; dress and behave with decorum.

UZBEKISTAN
Capital: Tashkent
Travel tips: roads are poor; beware photographing sensitive establishments; take adequate medical insurance and precautions.

VIETNAM
Capital: Hanoi
Travel tips: some areas have unexploded mines, etc.; take adequate medical insurance and precautions; drug laws are strictly enforced.

YEMEN
Capital: Saní

Travel tips: check on local security before travel and obtain clearance from your government.

2. AFRICA

The second-largest continent, with a total area of about 30,365,000 square kilometres, Africa has a coastline of about 28,000km. Much of Africa is tropical; the equator cuts the continent almost equally in two.

ALGERIA
Capital: Algiers
Travel tips: internal tensions have made this a high-risk zone; seek advice before attempting to travel.

ANGOLA
Capital: Luanda
Travel tips: identification should be carried at all times; seek advice before attempting to travel to this country; make security arrangements if travel is necessary.

BOTSWANA
Capital: Gaborone
Travel tips: rising unemployment has led to some rioting.

CAMEROON
Capital: Yaoundé
Travel tips: take advice on regional security; take sensible medical precautions, especially with regard to malaria.

CENTRAL AFRICAN REPUBLIC
Capital: Bangui
Travel tips: check on regional security before attempting travel; obtain clearance from your government; take sensible medical precautions, especially with regard to malaria.

CHAD
Capital: Ndjamena
Travel tips: check internal security, especially in border areas before travelling; take medical precautions, especially with regard to malaria.

CONGO, REPUBLIC OF
Capital: Brazzaville
Travel tips: tensions and violence between government and militias make it advisable to check on internal security before travelling and obtain clearance from your government if travel is absolutely necessary.

CÔTE D'IVOIRE
Capital: Yamoussoukro
Travel tips: take sensible medical precautions before travelling; standard of driving and of roads is poor; beware dangerous bathing.

EGYPT
Capital: Cairo
Travel tips: check on regional security before travelling; dress and behave with decorum; beware unexploded land mines.

EQUATORIAL GUINEA
Capital: Malabo
Travel tips: beware walking alone after dark, and guard possessions carefully; take medical precautions with regard to malaria.

ERITREA
Capital: Asmara
Travel tips: check on regional security before attempting to travel; obtain clearance from your government if travel is absolutely necessary.

ETHIOPIA
Capital: Addis Ababa
Travel tips: a visa is normally required; check on regional security before attempting to travel.

GAMBIA
Capital: Banjul
Travel tips: drug laws are strictly enforced; check on internal security before travelling; standards of driving and of roads are poor.

GHANA
Capital: Accra
Travel tips: take medical precautions with regard to malaria; standards of driving and of roads are poor.

GUINEA
Capital: Conakry
Travel tips: take precautions with regard to malaria and other diseases; beware tensions, particularly in border areas.

KENYA
Capital: Nairobi
Travel tips: beware of a high incidence of muggings; check on internal security before travelling; take medical precautions with regard to malaria, cholera and other diseases.

LESOTHO
Capital: Maseru
Travel tips: check on internal security before travelling.

LIBERIA
Capital: Monrovia
Travel tips: check on internal security before travelling; obtain clearance from your government if travel is absolutely necessary.

LIBYA
Capital: Tripoli
Travel tips: be circumspect with regard to photography and local customs; alcohol is illegal.

MADAGASCAR
Capital: Antananarivo
Travel tips: take medical precautions with regard to cholera.

MALAWI
Capital: Lilongwe
Travel tips: beware robberies and muggings; don't fraternise with strangers; take medical precautions with regard to cholera and malaria, and beware contaminated drinking water.

MAURITIUS
Capital: Port Louis
Travel tips: take care with regard to local drug laws.

MOROCCO
Capital: Rabat
Travel tips: beware severe drug laws; avoid large gatherings; respect local religious customs.

MOZAMBIQUE
Capital: Maputo
Travel tips: take medical precautions with regard to cholera and malaria, and beware contaminated drinking water; it is advisable to travel in groups; do not go out after dark; beware unexploded mines, etc.

NAMIBIA
Capital: Windhoek
Travel tips: check on regional security before travelling; take medical precautions with regard to malaria.

NIGERIA
Capital: Abuja
Travel tips: check on internal security before travelling; beware armed robbery and local disturbances.

RWANDA
Capital: Kigali
Travel tips: check on potential dangers from rebels, especially in border regions.

SENEGAL
Capital: Dakar
Travel tips: beware of border region with Guinea-Bissau; take medical precautions with regard to malaria.

SEYCHELLES
Capital: Victoria
Travel tips: take normal precautions with regard to possessions and do not go out alone especially after dark.

SIERRA LEONE
Capital: Freetown
Travel tips: there has been hostage taking of foreigners; do not travel unless given clearance by your government.

SOMALIA
Capital: Mogadishu
Travel tips: check on internal security before attempting to travel to this country.

SOUTH AFRICA
Capital: Pretoria & Cape Town
Travel tips: tourists are frequently targeted by pickpockets; also incidents of muggings and rape.

SUDAN
Capital: Khartoum
Travel tips: check on internal security before travel; beware unexploded landmines, etc.

SWAZILAND
Capital: Mbabane
Travel tips: do not fraternise with strangers; beware of poor standards of roads and driving.

TANZANIA
Capital: Dodoma
Travel tips: beware unrest in border areas; beware dangers of muggings and robberies; take medical precautions with regard to cholera and malaria, and beware contaminated drinking water.

TUNISIA
Capital: Tunis
Travel tips: drug laws are strictly enforced.

UGANDA
Capital: Kampala

Travel tips: a visa is normally required; obtain advice on which areas to avoid due to risk from bandits, local insurgents, etc.

ZAMBIA
Capital: Lusaka

Travel tips: a visa is normally required; strict drug laws; take medical precautions for cholera and malaria, and beware contaminated drinking water.

ZIMBABWE
Capital: Harare

Travel tips: beware petty crime and poor standard of roads and driving.

3. NORTH AND CENTRAL AMERICA

The third-largest continent has an area of about 24,230,000 square km.

BAHAMAS
Capital: Nassau

Travel tips: there is a risk of hurricanes in this area.

BELIZE
Capital: Belmopan

Travel tips: take medical precautions, especially with cholera.

CUBA
Capital: Havana

Travel tips: drug laws are strictly enforced; beware taking photographs of sensitive installations.

DOMINICAN REPUBLIC
Capital: Santo Domingo

Travel tips: be vigilant after dark; take care with drinking water.

EL SALVADOR
Capital: San Salvador

Travel tips: beware robberies, muggings and murders; take care with drinking water.

GUATEMALA
Capital: Guatemala City

Travel tips: drug laws are strictly enforced; beware robberies.

HAITI
Capital: Port-au-Prince

Travel tips: beware robberies and muggings.

HONDURAS
Capital: Tegucigalpa
Travel tips: beware robberies and muggings; take care with drinking water; high-risk hurricane area.

JAMAICA
Capital: Kingston
Travel tips: drug laws are strictly enforced; beware travelling alone after dark/robberies.

NICARAGUA
Capital: Managua
Travel tips: take medical precautions with regard to cholera and malaria, and beware contaminated drinking water; check on internal security, especially in border areas.

PANAMA
Capital: Panama City
Travel tips: beware unrest and danger of kidnapping in border areas.

4. SOUTH AMERICA

The fourth-largest continent has an area of about 17,814,000 square km and a coastline of about 40,922 square km.

ARGENTINA
Capital: Buenos Aires
Travel tips: beware street crime/ robberies, etc.

BOLIVIA
Capital: La Paz/Sucre
Travel tips: beware of health difficulties caused by high altitude; beware street crime; drug laws are strictly enforced.

BRAZIL
Capital: Brasília
Travel tips: take medical precautions, especially with regard to cholera; beware street crime, especially at night.

CHILE
Capital: Santiago
Travel tips: keep abreast of political developments in order to assess risk.

COLOMBIA
Capital: Bogotá
Travel tips: drug laws are strictly enforced; check on internal security with regard to the activities of guerrillas etc. before internal travel.

ECUADOR
Capital: Quito
Travel tips: this is a high-risk volcano area; drug laws are strictly enforced; carry personal identification with you; take sensible medical precautions.

PARAGUAY
Capital: Asunción
Travel tips: keep up to date with internal and regional security; beware problems with insurgents in border areas.

PERU
Capital: Lima
Travel tips: beware of problems associated with high altitude; take medical precautions, particularly with regard to malaria; drug laws are strictly enforced; do not travel alone unless absolutely necessary.

URUGUAY
Capital: Montevideo
Travel tips: beware street crime, and guard possessions carefully.

VENEZUELA
Capital: Caracas

Travel tips: a high risk of mud slides and similar natural disasters; there has been a rise in crime and drug trafficking; beware problems with drug traffickers in border areas.

5. EUROPE

The area of Europe is about 10,400,000 square km. with a coastline about 38,000 km long.

ALBANIA
Capital: Tirana
Travel tips: keep up to date with internal and regional security; standards of driving and of roads are poor; take care with contaminated local drinking water.

BELARUS
Capital: Minsk
Travel tips: a visa is normally required; take particular care with drinking water and food.

BOSNIA AND HERCEGOVINA
Capital: Sarajevo
Travel tips: beware unexploded mines, etc.

BULGARIA
Capital: Sofia
Travel tips: standards of roads and of driving are poor.

CROATIA
Capital: Zagreb
Travel tips: take advice on medical precautions; check on which areas to avoid due to risk from unexploded mines, etc.

CZECH REPUBLIC
Capital: Prague
Travel tips: carry personal identification at all times; take advice on necessary medical precautions.

ESTONIA
Capital: Talinn
Travel tips: personal identification must be carried at all times; standards of roads and of driving are poor.

GREECE
Capital: Athens
Travel tips: take out medical and travel insurance.

HUNGARY
Capital: Budapest
Travel tips: personal identification must be carried at all times.

ICELAND
Capital: Reykjavik
Travel tips: vehicles should have snow tyres, and check on state of internal routes, which may quickly become blocked with snow.

LATVIA
Capital: Riga
Travel tips: personal identification must be carried at all times; do not go out alone at night unless absolutely necessary.

LITHUANIA
Capital: Vilnius
Travel tips: do not go out after dark alone in poorly lit areas.

POLAND
Capital: Warsaw
Travel tips: standards of roads and of driving are poor.

ROMANIA
Capital: Bucharest
Travel tips: a visa is normally required; standards of roads and of

driving are poor; do not hand over personal documents unless in a police station.

SLOVAKIA
Capital: Bratislava
Travel tips: carry identification with you at all times.

SLOVENIA
Capital: Ljubljana
Travel tips: carry identification with you at all times.

UKRAINE
Capital: Kiev
Travel tips: a visa is normally required; carry identification with you at all times; beware drinking water.

7. AUSTRALASIA

Australia itself is the smallest continent with an area of about 8,000,000 square km. The coastline is 25,760 km.

AUSTRALIA
Capital: Canberra
Travel tips: beware flash floods and bush fires; do not travel alone after dark.

PAPUA NEW GUINEA
Capital: Port Moresby
Travel tips: a visa is normally required; be extremely vigilant about possible attacks; this is a volcano high risk area.

INDEX

Page references in *italics* refer to illustrations.